786434

First published July 1978

© THE INSTITUTE OF ECONOMIC AFFAIRS 1978

All rights reserved

ISSN 0073-2818

ISBN 0-255 36113-0

Printed in England by
GORON PRO-PRINT CO LTD,
6 Marlborough Road, Churchill Industrial Estate, Lancing, W. Sussex

Text set in 'Monotype' Baskerville

How Japan Competes

An assessment of international trading practices with special reference to 'dumping'

G. C. ALLEN

Emeritus Professor of Political Economy,
University of London

With a Commentary by

YUKIHIDE OKANO

Professor of Economics,
University of Tokyo

Published by

THE INSTITUTE OF ECONOMIC AFFAIRS

1978

IEA PUBLICATIONS

Subscription Service

An annual subscription is the most convenient way to obtain our publications. Every title we produce in our regular series will be sent to you immediately on publication and without further charge, representing a substantial saving.

Subscription rates

Britain: £10.00 p.a. including postage, reduced to £9.50 p.a. if paid by Banker's Order.

£7.50 p.a. to students and also to teachers who pay *personally.* No reduction for Banker's Orders.

Europe: 30 US dollars or equivalent.

North America: 35 US dollars.

Other countries: Rates on application. In many countries subscriptions are handled by local agents.

These rates are *not* available to companies or to institutions.

To: The Treasurer,
    Institute of Economic Affairs,
    2 Lord North Street,
    Westminster, London SW1P 3LB.

I should like an individual subscription beginning ....
I enclose a cheque/postal order for:

☐ £10.00
☐ £7.50 [student/teacher at ....]
☐ Please send me a Banker's Order form
☐ Please send me an Invoice

Name..

Address ....

....

Signed..   Date..................

HP81

How Japan Competes:
A Verdict on 'Dumping'
G. C. ALLEN

1. Japan's growing excess of exports over imports of goods in her trade with Britain has given rise to demands for selective import restrictions on them.

2. Japan's share of the British market for a few products (e.g. motor vehicles and electronic goods) is relatively high, but her total sales to Britain account for well under 3 per cent of Britain's imports. Moreover, the imbalance is largely redressed by Britain's surplus of 'invisibles' in her trade with Japan.

3. It is irrational to focus attention on bilateral balances. What is significant is the global, multilateral balance of payments. During the last two years Japan's world surplus on current account has brought difficulties to the international monetary system.

4. Japan's surplus is the result of a rapid expansion in her exports of goods unaccompanied by an equivalent growth in imports of goods and services. The imbalance is attributed by some of her competitors to 'unfair' practices in promoting exports and restricting imports.

5. During the 1950s and much of the 1960s these charges were well founded, but such practices have now been discarded to a large extent and probably play a smaller part in Japan's trade than in that of most Western countries.

6. The chief reason for Japan's competitive strength is that her industrial productivity has been increasing faster than that of other nations.

7. The remedy is not to be sought in restrictions on Japan's trade, for these might set going illiberal trends in international trade and retard recovery from the world recession.

8. The solution is likely to be found in a rise in the exchange value of the yen and the re-structuring of her economy as Japan emerges from her domestic recession.

9. Japan will probably direct more of her investment into the economic and social infrastructure and less into manufacturing industry, and consumption will make up more of her national expenditure and investment less. These changes, if accompanied by import liberalisation, should enlarge the business of foreign exporters to Japan, if they seize their opportunities.

10. The rest of the world also ought to be prepared to re-allocate its resources in response to Japan's superior efficiency in some branches of manufacture. Consumers will then be able to enjoy to the full the benefits of Japan's technological and commercial progress.

Hobart Paper 81 is published price (£1·50) by

THE INSTITUTE OF ECONOMIC AFFAIRS
2 Lord North Street, Westminster
London SW1P 3LB . Telephone: 01-799 3745

CONTENTS

[3]

A JAPANESE COMMENTARY
by
Yukihide Okano

[4]

[5]

PREFACE

The *Hobart Papers* are intended to contribute a stream of authoritative, independent and lucid analysis to the understanding and application of economics to private and government activity. Their characteristic theme has been the optimum use of scarce resources and the extent to which it can best be achieved in markets within an appropriate framework of laws and institutions or, where markets cannot work or have disproportionate defects, by better methods with relative advantages or less decisive defects. Since the alternative to the market is in practice the state, and both are imperfect, the choice between them is effectively made on the judgement of the comparative consequences of 'market failure' and 'government failure'.

One of the markets of which competitors have most anxiously complained has been the international market between countries with supposedly different industrial backgrounds and costs. Here the most celebrated example is that of Japan, which has been competing more strongly with Britain and Europe in recent years and which is accused of aggressive marketing, not least by selling exports at less than their 'cost' while, at the same time, restricting the access of foreign producers to its home market. This argument has recently led to increasing calls and pressures for a tariff and other 'protection' against Japanese imports of a wide range of consumer goods against which, it is argued, British industry cannot compete on equal or 'fair' terms.

This proposition is examined in Hobart Paper 81 by Professor G. C. Allen, a distinguished and respected economic authority on the industry and trade of Japan. He examines the economics of the Japanese economy without bias, with restraint, and with a cool-headed determination to arrive at the truth. In brief, he concludes that, although some practices would not be used in Britain or Europe and others might be justifiably described as misleading, the success of Japanese industry in competing with British and European industry, despite long distances and high transport costs, is due essentially

[7]

not to her trading practices but to her superior industrial efficiency.

The corollary that Professor Allen discusses, the inability of British industry to compete in Japanese markets, reflects the failure of British industrialists, management and trade unions to display the enterprise, initiative and efficiency of the Japanese.

The Institute's usual practice is to have early drafts of its *Papers* read by two or more economists. In this case they were Mr Gilbert J. Ponsonby, who offered observations on the general argument that have been taken into account in the final revisions, and Professor Yukihide Okano, of the University of Tokyo, who fortuitously was on a spell of study at the University of Oxford. Professor Okano's lengthy series of comments were considered so interesting and valuable that, at Professor Allen's suggestion, they have been added to form a Commentary. We thank Mr Ponsonby and Professor Okano for their comments and suggestions.

Professor Allen's *Hobart Paper* should help to encourage a cooler analysis of the reasons for the success of competition from Japanese imports. It should therefore direct attention away from supposed solutions like protection, which would leave the comparative weakness of British industry untouched. It should instead direct attention to the more fundamental causes of these weaknesses and, by stimulating thought on methods of removing them, indirectly help to strengthen British industry.

The constitution of the Institute requires it to dissociate its Trustees, Directors and Advisers from the argument and conclusions of its authors. The Institute presents this *Hobart Paper* by one of its eminent Trustees as a scholarly, urbane, and clearly-written analysis of a subject that has caused not only heated and unenlightened public discussion but also misguided thinking from economists, mostly at Cambridge, who have not similarly analysed the reasons for the differences in the relative efficiency of British and Japanese industry.

June 1978   ARTHUR SELDON

THE AUTHOR

G. C. ALLEN is Emeritus Professor of Political Economy, University of London. Born in 1900 and educated at King Henry VIII School, Coventry, and the University of Birmingham, where he was a Research Fellow and Lecturer, 1925-29; Lecturer in Economics at the Higher Commercial College, Nagoya, Japan, 1922-25; Professor of Economics and Commerce, University College, Hull, 1929-33; Brunner Professor of Economic Science, University of Liverpool, 1933-47; and finally Professor of Political Economy, University College, London, 1947-67. He was President of the Economics Section, British Association, in 1950; a member of the Monopolies Commission, 1950 to 1962. Author of books on industrial and economic development, including *Monopoly and Restrictive Practices* (1968) and *Japan's Economic Expansion* (1965). He has also written two well-known textbooks on the structure of British industry; *British Industries and their Organisation* (1933, revised edn. 1970), and *The Structure of Industry in Britain* (1961, revised edn. 1970).

For the IEA, of which he is a Trustee, Professor Allen has written *Economic Fact and Fantasy* (Occasional Paper 14, 1967, 2nd edn. 1969); an essay, 'Competition and Mergers', in *Mergers, Take-overs and the Structure of Industry* (IEA Readings No. 10, 1973); Part II of *The Price of Prosperity: Lessons from Japan* (Hobart Paper 58, 1974); and *The British Disease* (Hobart Paper 67, 1976).

YUKIHIDE OKANO

Professor of Economics, University of Tokyo. Born in 1929 and educated at the University of Tokyo, where he obtained his MA, and at the University of Chicago, 1960-63. Research Associate (*Joshu*), 1964-66, Associate Professor (*Jokyoju*), 1966-76, and Professor since 1976 at the University of Tokyo. Visiting Research Fellow at St Antony's College and Transport Studies Unit, University of Oxford, 1977-79. Author or editor of books on transport economics and policy, public utilities and public economics, including *The Economics of Transport* (1977), *Lectures on Transport Economics* (1975), and (with Takashi Negishi as co-editor) *Public Economics* (1973). He has contributed to the Japanese professional periodicals, including *Transportation Studies, Journal of Economics,* and *Quarterly Journal of Economic Studies.*

[9]

AUTHOR'S ACKNOWLEDGEMENTS

I have been greatly helped by the information, including much documentary material, provided by the Commercial Relations and Export Division, Department of Trade; the Information Centre of the Japanese Embassy (London); and the Anglo-Japanese Economic Institute, London. I am very grateful to the officials or members of these bodies for the trouble they have taken. I also wish to thank my friend, Mr A. Morikawa a businessman of Urawa City, Japan, for much valuable assistance.

June 1978   G.C.A.

I. INTRODUCTION: DOES JAPAN TRADE RUTHLESSLY?

In the course of her modern economic development Japan has been frequently accused by her trading partners of employing 'unfair' trading practices, including dumping in overseas markets and discrimination against foreign competitors in her home market. Those who have suffered from her competition have not been slow to appeal to their governments for protection or retaliatory measures, and the world recession has made them more importunate than ever.

In recent years the appearance of a succession of very large surpluses in Japan's balance of payments on current account seems to provide evidence in support of the contention that she has entirely disregarded the interests of her trading partners in pursuit of her own economic ambitions. The purpose of this *Hobart Paper* is to examine those charges and to consider whether her success in international trade is attributable to 'unfair' methods and whether Western governments and industrialists have a justifiable grievance.

The post-war pattern of Japanese trade

We must first review the course of Japanese foreign trade since the Second World War and consider how the present imbalance came about.

Japan's remarkable success as an exporter and her huge payments surpluses are of recent origin. Her export trade had been completely destroyed by the war and her chief markets—for raw silk in the United States and for cotton textiles and other light manufactured goods in China—had been permanently lost.

Throughout the 1950s the revival of her exports was much slower than the revival of her production, and it was not until 1959 (when industrial production was nearly three times higher than before the war) that the volume of exports exceeded that of the middle 1930s. It was even later, in 1963, that Japan regained the share in world exports she had held before the war. Japan's current account was in frequent deficit until the late 1960s, and her monetary authorities had been obliged on several occasions to put a brake on her industrial recovery to meet a deterioration in the balance of payments.

This protracted anxiety about the country's financial position had a profound and lasting effect on the government and the business community which survived long after the cause had disappeared. Throughout the 1960s, despite the country's exceptionally rapid economic growth and an export trade which increased twice as fast as world trade, the attitude of Japanese business men and officials towards their country's economic and financial future remained pessimistic. It is no exaggeration to say that Japan, by this time highly developed industrially, retained the outlook of an under-developed country.

The persistence of this attitude may be explained by the suddenness of the change in the country's international financial position from chronic deficit to surplus. The succession of surpluses on current account began in 1968, with an upward surge in exports, and it continued until the 'oil shock' of 1973 raised the import bill and again put the account into deficit. This reversal seemed to justify the view that the period of surplus had been temporary and that Japan was entering upon another period of financial difficulty. Even Professor Kiyoshi Kojima, an expert on international trade, affirmed, in a book written in 1975,[1] that there was no likelihood of a return to the large surpluses of 1968-72. Yet, by the end of 1975, Japan had already gone far towards adjusting her economy to the increased price of oil. In 1976 her exports of goods grew by 21 per cent in value, while, because of the domestic recession, imports made a much smaller increase of 12 per cent. The growth, and the disparity, continued into 1977, when the surpluses on both trade and current accounts were massive.[2] The gap has, of course, been filled by capital movements, partly by an increase in Japan's short-term and long-term investments, and partly by a steep rise in her reserves of gold and foreign exchange.

[1] K. Kojima, *Japan and a New World Order,* Croom Helm, London, 1977, p. 38.

[2] Table I, p. 54. In 1976 Japan exported *in volume* 47 per cent more than in 1973; the *volume* of her imports fell by nearly 6 per cent in this period. It should be emphasised that comparisons of the trade in *value* over the last two years have become difficult because of the fall in the value of the dollar in which the exports and imports are given in many international trade statistics (Tables I and II).

Trade with the US: the 'Nixon shock', 1971

Throughout most of the post-war period Japan's chief markets were North America, especially the United States, and South-East and South Asia. In 1965 these two groups of markets took nearly two-thirds of the exports. Europe's share was only 13 per cent, including the United Kingdom's 2·4 per cent. Up to this time European manufacturers had met with some competition from the Japanese in overseas markets, but, except in textiles, they had suffered little at home. The largest item in Japan's sales to Europe and the UK then consisted of foodstuffs. When her rapid export advance began in the later 1960s, it was first directed towards the United States. As Japan's purchases from the USA failed to increase as rapidly as her exports, a large imbalance appeared for the first time in that trade. In 1971 Japan's surplus on her trade with the United States reached 3·2 billion dollars, much larger than the total American trade deficit in that year. The Americans responded by introducing new restrictions on imports from Japan and, in August 1971, they depreciated the dollar, an event referred to by the Japanese as the 'Nixon shock'.

The effect of this check to trade expansion in their chief market for manufactures was to divert part of the export effort to other countries, and it was then that Japan's sales to Europe began to expand. In 1976-77 Japan sent nearly 18 per cent of her exports to Europe, compared with about 15 per cent in 1971,[1] when the absolute size of the export trade was much smaller. As the rise in Europe's exports to Japan did not nearly match her imports from Japan, the trade became heavily unbalanced. Until 1968 there had been no significant disparity; but by 1976 and 1977 Japan exported to Europe more than twice the amount she bought. The trade surplus rose to over 7 billion dollars in 1976 and to nearly 9 billion dollars in 1977. Britain, taken alone, shared the same experience. During the 1960s the trade balance had been only slightly in Japan's favour, but in 1976 there was a surplus of 560 million dollars in a total Japan-Britain commodity trade of 2·26 billion dollars.[2] It is to this imbalance, the failure of Japan to

[1] Excluding the USSR. Exports are valued f.o.b., imports c.i.f.

[2] In 1977, when the total value of the trade came to 2·9 billion dollars, Japan's favourable trade balance with Britain reached nearly 1 billion dollars. But note that the dollar depreciated in 1977 by nearly a quarter in terms of yen.

[13]

match her rising sales by equivalently large purchases, that can be attributed much of the outcry in Europe against her advance. In this respect Europe has followed the United States which was the first industrial country on the receiving end of Japan's export drive. The 'outcry', of course, has come from governments and producers. Consumers have apparently welcomed with enthusiasm the goods the Japanese have offered to them. (The interests of British consumers are discussed at several points below.)

Is Japanese trade 'unfair'?

For Western countries as a whole, Japan's trade advance has been the more damaging to domestic manufacturers because it has been concentrated on a rather narrow front. In 1976 her total exports to Europe and the United States rose by nearly 35 per cent over those for 1975. The average conceals the enormous increase for particular products: 94 per cent for cold strip steel, 87 per cent for colour TV sets, 68 per cent for radios, 64 per cent for ships, 60 per cent for steel bars and shapes, and 49 per cent for motor vehicles. Hence the alarm and resentment of the Western manufacturing industries which bore the brunt of this competition. The Europeans have perhaps been even more resentful than the Americans, because of a special characteristic of their trade with Japan. In her other large markets (South-East Asia, West Asia, Australia, Africa, South America and even the United States) Japan's trade is predominantly 'vertical' (the exchange of manufactures for raw materials, food and fuel), but with Europe her trade is now 'horizontal' (the exchange of manufactures). For this reason, Europe, as a highly developed industrial region, is said to find the increasing imbalance especially intolerable. By 'Europe' one must understand 'the European industries suffering from Japanese competition'. European consumers obviously have had no complaints; they have been eager to buy Japanese products.

The Japanese have made several ripostes to these criticisms. First, they emphasise Japan's extreme dependence on imports of raw materials, fuel and (increasingly) food because of her lack of natural resources; in this respect Japan compares unfavourably with Western European countries, and still more so with the United States. Inevitably, therefore, only a small share of the total imports is left for manufactures—20 per cent

[14]

compared with about 50 per cent for most other large industrial countries.[1]

Second, the Japanese insist that their large and growing surplus on visible trade has been offset to a large extent, if not wholly, in their dealings with Europe, and particularly with the UK, by a corresponding deficit on invisibles. The size of this deficit and its significance are open to argument. What Europe earns bilaterally on her invisible trade with Japan cannot be regarded as a net gain, for these transactions often give rise to outward payments in dealings with third countries. This problem is, of course, met with in attempts to estimate bilateral visible trade balances also, and it is unlikely that interested parties will ever reach agreement about the dimensions of the imbalances. For instance, on a Japanese calculation, Britain's surplus on invisibles with Japan in 1975 was £650 million, whereas the British authorities put it at only £250 million.[2]

It is, of course, irrational to focus attention on bilateral balances, visible or invisible; what is significant is a country's current balance in her transactions with the world as a whole, although even then capital transactions intrude to complicate any policy judgement. We should certainly have heard less of Japan's imbalance with Europe but for the contribution it makes to her large and growing surplus with the whole community of her trading partners.

The Japanese riposte: UK discriminates against them

The Japanese have not been slow to point out that, although Britain's trade deficits with several European countries are considerably larger than with Japan, the British Government has not made any complaint about *them*. In the last three years Japan's contribution to Britain's deficit has ranged between only 3·7 and 8·5 per cent of the total, compared with 9·7 to 17·8 per cent for Holland and 13·2 to 16·9 per cent for West Germany.[3] 'Why', ask the Japanese, 'should Britain's resent-

---

[1] The 20 per cent applies to the period since 1973. During the 1960s and early 1970s the proportion had been rising and reached about 30 per cent in 1972. The decline in the proportion after 1972 is to be explained by the hugely enhanced cost of Japan's oil imports.

[2] Japan Information Centre, *British Trade with Japan*, London, January 1977, pp. 6, 10 and 11.

[3] Britain's deficits in her trade with Canada, Saudi Arabia and Iran have also been much larger than her deficits with Japan.

[15]

ment be concentrated on us?' Their answer to this question goes far towards explaining their reluctance to abandon some features of their trading policy that have excited the most bitter criticism. They are not yet convinced that they have been completely accepted as members of the community of developed nations. They think that the British disposition to single them out as offenders against the principles of good-neighbourly trading proves the justice of their criticism, since others share their fault, if fault it is.

The circumstances attending the 'Nixon shock' in 1971 and other international episodes since then suggest that the Japanese cannot expect the same considerate treatment in times of crisis as Western nations extend to each other. They are thus persuaded that a self-regarding policy is not without justification. They cannot afford hastily to abandon ways that have served them well in order to meet the criticisms of an international trading community that still looks askance at their enterprise.

Moreover, the events of the last few years have warned them to be cautious. The steep deterioration in their terms of trade after 1973, the consequence of the rise in oil prices, was obviously not conducive to the diversion of their energies from the export drive. In 1976 the Japanese had to export 45 per cent more goods, in quantity, than in 1973 in order to buy the same quantity of imports. Yet, despite this worsening in their terms of trade, they have shown themselves willing to advance rapidly in the direction of a more liberal trading policy. The main incentive has been the recognition by the Japanese Government that their future prosperity depends on the expansion of world trade and that they must do nothing to strengthen the trend towards protectionism caused by the general recession after 1974.

II. DISCRIMINATORY TRADE PRACTICES: 'DUMPING'

To what extent have Japan's exports been stimulated and her imports discouraged by 'unfair' or discriminatory trading practices? Of all the charges brought against her, that of 'dumping' has been the most persistent. The term is used very loosely in commercial controversy, and for the purpose of this *Paper* it is necessary to define the meanings that can be given to it.

'Social dumping' in the 1930s?

During the 1930s, when Japan's exports made a remarkable advance, though international trade was stagnating, her success was widely attributed to what was called 'social dumping'. This charge rested not simply on her very low wages by the standards of her Western competitors, but also on the proposition that she had deliberately depressed the living standards of large groups of her workers to increase her exports.[1] This proposition was supported by evidence of falling real wages in the affected industries.[2]

It is now generally agreed that Japan's trade expansion at that time was made possible by her accepting increasingly unfavourable terms of trade and that the burden was carried mainly by workers in the export industries.[3] In this sense one can agree that there was 'social dumping'. We need not try to decide whether the deterioration was the result of a deliberate policy designed to promote political ambitions overseas, or whether it was mainly the consequence of the collapse in the demand for her chief export commodity (raw silk) in the World Depression.

Whatever the cause, consumers abroad undoubtedly benefited by this 'social dumping', not least the impoverished peoples of

---

[1] Particularly in the textiles and miscellaneous consumption goods industries.

[2] T. Uyeda, *The Small Industries of Japan*, Oxford University Press, 1938, pp. 287-304.

[3] The terms of trade worsened by 40 per cent between 1931 and 1937, according to M. Shinohara, *Growth and Cycles in the Japanese Economy*, Kenkyusha, Tokyo, 1962, p. 85.

East and South-East Asia who gave a ready welcome to imports of cheap Japanese consumption goods.

The relief of Asian poverty by Japan's commercial enterprise, however, brought little satisfaction to those Western manufacturing firms (chiefly producers of textiles) whose products had been displaced by the competition; nor to Western governments whose difficulties in contending with the problem of localised unemployment were enhanced by the damage inflicted on certain of their established industries. In countries such as Britain where there was structural rigidity, that problem proved to be especially intractable. The plight of their most seriously affected trades persuaded several Western governments to impose restrictions on Japanese imports into their home market and to discriminate against them in their colonies. The restrictions, of course, did nothing to prevent 'social dumping'; and they probably worsened the conditions of workers in the Japanese export industries.

These consequences we need not now explore since, for our present purpose, the importance of the pre-war phase of Japanese competition, and of the Western response to it, lies in its effect on post-war attitudes to which reference has been made. Nevertheless, it should be emphasised that the political consequences were very serious, for the restrictions justified, in the eyes of many Japanese, their government's policy of imperialist expansion.[1]

Japanese pre- and post-war trade

Japan's post-war return to world markets occurred in very different conditions from those of the 1930s. For one thing, the economic environment had been transformed. In place of stagnation in international trade, there was buoyancy throughout the 1950s and 1960s; indeed world trade rose even faster than the world's GNP. In the second place, when Japan emerged from her period of recovery, it was seen that she was no longer, as in pre-war times, a country of peasant agriculture with a fringe of labour-intensive industries, with low wages and little capital. By 1970 she had become the second largest industrial country in the non-Communist world; her industrial structure closely resembled that of the leading Western states. Her technology had reached European and American stan-

---

[1] G. C. Allen, *Japan, The Hungry Guest,* Allen and Unwin, 1938, pp. 201, 235-36.

dards in all but a few industries, and the earnings of her workers were almost equal to those of the most prosperous Europeans.

In the early post-war years, Western textile manufacturers had been troubled by the resurgence of Japanese competition, as her industrial reconstruction began with textiles. Their fears of this competition, as we shall see, influenced commercial policy towards her textile exports for many years to come. With the rise of her new capital-intensive industries, the chief anxieties of her competitors shifted to other products, and, by the 1960s, Japanese textile industries were themselves threatened by the supply of cheap goods from the newly developing countries.

During the last decade and a half, the products which have made up the bulk of Japan's exports have consisted of steel, ships, electrical and electronic apparatus, organic chemicals, machinery and motor cars. As these are the very products in which Europeans and Americans had hitherto shown their distinctive excellence as manufacturers, it can easily be understood why Western governments and industrialists have been ready to attribute Japan's export successes to 'unfair' trading practices, including dumping. They have also ascribed their failure to make headway in Japan's home market to the restrictive policies of the Japanese Government, or to the discriminatory devices of industrialists and traders.

The economics of 'dumping'

Dumping occurs when a producer sells his goods at lower prices abroad than at home, after allowance for cost-differences in serving the two markets. It is a form of price discrimination and depends on the existence of distinct markets with differing elasticities of demand (that is to say, demand in some markets is more responsive to a change in price than it is in others). The producer who 'dumps' must be able to charge an 'administered' price in his home market (because he enjoys a measure of monopoly there), whereas in the foreign markets, where he has to face competition, he is normally a 'price-taker'.

In the classical theory of dumping, three types are distinguished: sporadic, persistent and predatory.

(i) *Sporadic dumping*

A priori, one might suppose that sporadic dumping (which includes the efforts of producers to clear their stocks or to

[19]

maintain production during a domestic recession by selling at low prices abroad) is that most likely to have been practised by Japanese firms. It is well known that periods of domestic recession in Japan have often been associated with a sharp rise in exports (by volume, not necessarily by value). This association has been in some degree the consequence of the financial structure of Japanese industry. Until recently the typical firm has depended on bank loans to finance its expansion and has been under strong pressure to maintain production, even in recessions, to service its loans.[1] Whether the rise in exports at such times was achieved by dumping or simply by Japanese firms adapting themselves to changing circumstances can be shown only by evidence which is unfortunately difficult to obtain.

(ii) *Persistent dumping*

Persistent dumping can be practised only if the producer enjoys a well-entrenched monopoly in his own market. Such a monopoly may come into being without the intervention of government. But where official policy is intent upon import-substitution and the stimulation of exports, trade and foreign exchange regulations may be framed so as to penalise competitive imports and to subsidise exports. In such circumstances price differentials may be disguised by manipulation.

For Japan the importance, in the past, of official trade and exchange regulations can hardly be exaggerated. Japan's post-war economy has been highly competitive, a condition characteristic not only of the large small-firm sector, but also of the big conglomerates.[2] Cartels have led a precarious existence and 'weak sellers' soon appear whenever domestic demand falters.[3] In the absence of trade and exchange regulations, therefore, sustained monopolistic pricing by the majority of producers would have been difficult. The trade and exchange regulations and their administration are thus very pertinent to this inquiry.

(iii) *Predatory dumping*

Predatory dumping occurs when a firm sells abroad cheaply

---

[1] Another reason is indicated in the footnote to p. 47.

[2] The intense rivalry between conglomerates is consistent with a disposition on the part of members of particular conglomerates to give some degree of preference to fellow-members in placing contracts (p. 38).

[3] Because of their weak financial position, or for other reasons, some members of cartels can often be induced by customers to cut their prices below those fixed by the cartels.

with the intention of destroying an existing or a potential source of alternative supply. Japan has been accused seldom, if ever, of 'predatory' dumping, although the line between predatory dumping and the measures employed by a newcomer to break into a market dominated by established producers is thin. A discriminatory price policy is often introduced as the first stage in an attack of this sort and is a commonplace of competition among large firms in all countries; it is, of course, difficult to identify and usually impossible to prohibit.

III. JAPANESE TRADE POLICY IN THE 1950s AND 1960s

For the first part of the 1950s exports lagged behind the rate of industrial growth, and the imports that made that growth possible were financed largely by the United States' special procurement expenditure.[1] It became a prime objective of Japanese policy to stimulate exports and to limit imports to what were deemed essential for industrial rehabilitation. Hence all foreign exchange and trading transactions were subject to stringent controls.

An illustration of the devices then employed is the 'link' system, in which import licences for particular commodities were given by the authorities on condition that the licensee exported a specified amount of manufactured goods. (The great trading firms are all two-way traders.) The disparity between the foreign and domestic prices of the imports enabled the licensee to make a profit on the transaction. This could be used to reduce the price he charged for the exports which were a condition of obtaining the licence. Tax discrimination was exercised in favour of export industries, and export bills were discounted at low rates of interest through the Central Bank. Associations of exporters were set up under the Export-Import Trading Act of 1953 with the express object of dumping goods abroad. Some of these associations raised levies on the sales of their members in the home market in order to provide the means for subsidising exports. Meanwhile imports remained tightly controlled by quantitative quotas and by the central allocation of foreign exchange (discussed further below, pp. 24, 31).

Western complaints muted during re-building of Japan's economy

During the 1950s the complaints of Japan's trading partners about her trading methods were muted. It was recognised that her international financial position was weak because her reconstruction had not yet been completed, and that the methods she was using to strengthen it were understandable, if

---

[1] Includes US military expenditure in dollars, yen purchases for Joint Defence Account, expenditure of American soldiers and civilians in Japan and payments for off-shore contracts.

not always justified. The United States, the chief objective of the export drive, looked to Japan to provide her with a stable military base in the Far East and was anxious to assist in re-building her economy. Europe was indifferent, since its industries had not yet suffered seriously from Japanese competition (except in textiles) and it had shown little interest in Japan as a market.

Western industrial countries had, however, already taken some steps to safeguard themselves against the possible return of Japanese competition which, they assumed, would take its pre-war form. Japan's admission to the General Agreement on Tariffs and Trade (GATT) was at first opposed by several European countries. Eventually when she was allowed to join (in 1955), the contracting parties invoked Article XXXV, which gave them the right to waive their obligations to her in stated circumstances. Other forms of discrimination were practised against Japan, including quantitative restrictions on imports of named goods. Pressure was also applied by Western governments from time to time to persuade the Japanese Government to introduce 'voluntary' export controls.

In these negotiations the Americans seem to have led the way. From 1956, exports of Japanese cotton fabrics to the United States were covered by 'voluntary' quotas; in 1961-62 the arrangements were systematised by a multi-national agreement under the GATT which allotted export quotas to the various producing and exporting countries. The agreement was extended in 1963 to cover a wider range of textiles, but these restrictions, it is ironical to record, came into effect just when textiles were receding in importance among Japan's exports. They served to protect her own textile industries against imports from the developing countries rather than to fend off Japanese goods from the American market.

Other products were dealt with in the same way during the 1960s. In 1968 the US Government persuaded Japan to hold her steel exports at an agreed figure for that year. Recently, a voluntary agreement between producers in Japan and the EEC placed restrictions on the quantity of steel imports into Europe for 1977, and, under a 'standstill' arrangement, imports for 1978 are to be held to the 1977 level. The sales of Japanese stainless steel tableware, pottery, motor cars and electronic equipment to Britain have been affected by similar 'voluntary' restrictive agreements.

[23]

Abandonment of exchange controls

During the 1960s, under pressure from her trading partners, the elaborate structure of Japan's restrictions was gradually dismantled. She agreed, with some reluctance, to abandon exchange controls over current transactions (as required by Article 8 of the International Monetary Fund) and, after yielding to the demand that she should adopt Article 11 status under the GATT, she began to discard the quantitative restrictions on imports and to modify her methods of stimulating exports. The Japanese authorities claimed that, by the end of 1967, 93 per cent of their country's trade had been liberalised; but this figure has little significance since, in 1959 (the reference year for the calculation) many types of manufactures which overseas suppliers might have sold to Japan were not being imported at all because of the controls.

Liberalisation was much slower than the Japanese made it out to be, and in 1970 a quarter of the imports were still covered by quotas, although the quotas themselves had been enlarged during the preceding few years.[1] The Japanese urged in excuse that many of their own exports were still subject to onerous restrictions of a discriminatory kind. In 1971 they informed the GATT that the number of so-called 'voluntary' quota restrictions on her exports was 264. Other forms of restriction were also common, including the discriminatory licensing of imports by some countries. Very few of these restrictions could be justified by any proven charge of dumping.

Despite the discrimination, Japan's export trade had succeeded during the 1960s in growing twice as fast as world trade as a whole, and her trade surplus at the end of the decade suggested that the restrictions had had little effect on her competitive strength.

Liberalisation quickened after 1970

In these circumstances Japan could hardly resist the renewed pressure from her trading partners, and the pace of her liberalisation was accelerated after 1970. Today only foodstuffs and a few minor classes of manufactures remain covered by quantitative import controls.

During the same period her import duties on manufactures

[1] H. Kitamura, *Choices for the Japanese Economy*, Royal Institute of International Affairs, London, 1976, p. 144.

[24]

have been reduced, not only as a result of the Kennedy Round in 1964-67, but also by a unilateral reduction of 20 per cent in 1972. (This liberal action was, no doubt, intended to appease Western critics of her trade expansion.) In consequence, her duties (with a few exceptions) have been brought into line with those of Europe; indeed, they are lower than those of several of her trading partners.

In the subsidisation of exports, or 'persistent' dumping, Japan's recent record entitles her to claim that she is, if not blameless, less guilty than most of those countries which accuse her. The British sustain their iron and steel, shipbuilding and motor industries by lavish subsidies. The corresponding industries in Japan have lately flourished without any direct official subventions. Except in a few instances, recent charges of dumping have been impossible to prove. The modification of the protective devices that were a necessary condition of persistent dumping during the early post-war years has limited dumping to the few effectively cartelised industries.[1]

A residue of dumping?

It is not surprising that, in recent times, examples of dumping are hard to find, and that those where the evidence has been strong enough to warrant the imposition of anti-dumping duties are of minor importance.

1. In February 1977, for example, the EEC levied a 10-20 per cent anti-dumping duty for three months on imports of Japanese ball-bearings on the ground that they were being sold in Europe 26 per cent below the domestic Japanese price. In June 1977 it extended the period of the duty and fixed it at 15 per cent, even though the Japanese firms undertook to raise their export prices by 20 per cent. They are contesting the validity of this measure and are to bring the case before the International Court.

2. The British Government in May 1977 imposed a provisional anti-dumping duty of £15 a tonne on steel flats from Japan, but soon felt obliged to repeal the duty because it was shown that, despite some measure of dumping, its extent was

---

[1] But there is a qualification to this assertion (p. 27).

insufficient to justify an anti-dumping duty.[1] It may be contended that this type of steel and some others have been sold at under long-run average cost in the home market, but such a pricing practice cannot be regarded as dumping. Japan's steel industry has been working well under capacity, and in such circumstances it would be a rational business policy for a firm to sell at under full cost if it thereby loses less than by cutting production and holding prices. Competitive forces are difficult to curb in Japan since her cartels are usually ineffective,[2] which explains much of Japan's resilience and general economic efficiency.

3. The large increase in Japan's steel exports to the United States provoked the American producers to file charges of dumping with the US Treasury during the Spring and Summer of 1977.[3] Even if, as is doubtful, this charge could be proved, the legal proceedings would certainly be protracted, and it is probable that the dispute will be settled by another 'voluntary' agreement by the Japanese firms to curtail their exports.

These 'voluntary' agreements have often left the Japanese with a sense of grievance, since the result of restraint by them has in the past simply opened the way to imports from other countries. They have made this reply in connection with their agreement to limit their share of the British car market to 10 per cent. The benefit, they contend, has not gone to the British producers but to Continental European suppliers. In this case the question of dumping has not been raised.

The conclusion must be that, whatever was true of the 1950s and early 1960s, during recent years dumping has been responsible for only a small proportion of Japan's exports. It certainly cannot be regarded as having contributed significantly to her large trade surplus.

[1] According to the GATT anti-dumping code, anti-dumping duties cannot be imposed if the margin of competitiveness is very small; for steel flats the difference was only £2 to £3 a tonne.

[2] Except when authorised by government, as with the 'recession cartels' in textiles.

[3] Britain has been accused in Congress of the same offence. Indeed, her high-cost steel industry is alleged to have sold steel plate in the US cheaper than the Japanese, who are accused of having sold the product at 32 per cent below the home price. The British offence is deemed worse than that of the Japanese, for while the latter have not lately received government financial help, the British Steel Corporation has been given about £700 million in subsidies during the last three years. (*The Times*, Business Section, 5 November, 1977.)

Financial subsidies?

This important conclusion still leaves unresolved another problem which finds its roots in the subtle relations between government and private industry in Japan. The help accorded to exporters was not limited to direct subsidies. During the years immediately after the war, and indeed for much of the next decade, the reconstruction of Japanese industries, including those that became leading exporters, depended heavily on low-interest loans and other financial assistance from institutions closely associated with the government. At the end of the war firms were left with meagre resources of liquid capital and with their fixed assets run down. At first, the government's Reconstruction Finance Bank and the Counterpart Fund Special Account furnished the loans. Later this function was assumed by other official financial institutions, such as the Japan Development Bank, and by the commercial banks when they had built up their resources.

Throughout the whole period (the 1950s and 1960s) a key role in the country's economic development, including its export trade, was played by the central monetary authorities, whose directing power was derived from the extreme dependence of industry on bank credit to finance its expansion. After the early years of reconstruction the chief immediate source of such credit was the commercial banking sector; central control remained effective because the commercial banks relied on the central bank for funds to accommodate their clients.

The allocation of these credits has often been decided by the central government's economic policy rather than by independent market forces. Thus the rate of interest charged for the loans has been less decisive than 'window guidance', that is to say, decisions to grant or to refuse loans have been strongly influenced by official policy concerning the type of industrial activity in which the applicant proposed to engage. As this system still persists, it is impossible to discover whether or not certain exporting industries are receiving hidden subsidies through access to cheap bank credit, or preferential treatment.[1]

The question is relevant to the operations of the legally independent commercial banks, but it is raised in its most unequivocal form by the activities of the state banks which derive their resources in part from budgetary funds and in part

[1] During the 1970s the dependence of industrial firms on bank loans for financing *capital expenditure* was much reduced.

[27]

from postal savings.[1] In the lending decisions of the Export-Import Bank, for example, commercial criteria, it is acknowledged, usually take second place to political or administrative considerations. Japan is not, of course, unique in allocating credit in accordance with the central government's economic objectives. To the outside world, what is inexcusable is the benefit she has apparently gained from doing so!

Shipping and shipbuilding: a case study

A discussion limited to general principles must seem perfunctory. A particular group of industries, shipping and shipbuilding, may be taken as examples of the part played by the government and its financial agencies in industrial recovery and expansion.[2]

At the end of the war nearly all Japan's merchant ships were at the bottom of the sea and the shipbuilding and allied industries had lost much of their manufacturing capacity. The government bent itself to the task of reconstruction as soon as it was free to do so. From 1947 until 1962 a very high proportion of the orders for ships were placed under an official programme and were financed largely from funds borrowed from the government banks at less than commercial rates. By 1956 the policy had been so successful as to raise Japan into first place among the world's shipbuilders. After the middle 1950s, with the export boom, government-sponsored shipbuilding diminished in importance. Early in the 1960s, the government's participation was resumed. An official programme in 1962 accounted for over half the industry's orders for the domestic market, and this policy was vigorously pursued for several years. As late as 1972 the Annual Budget provided 120,000 million yen (about $400 million) for subsidising bank loans to shipowners.

Both in the early years of reconstruction and in the period in which Japanese shipbuilding attained its overwhelming predominance in the world, government subsidies, mainly in the form of low-interest loans, made an important contribution. Without this help the industry would probably have been unable to break into foreign markets, let alone dominate them. During the last decade, this official support has diminished.

[1] Via the Deposits Bureau of the Ministry of Finance.

[2] Seymour Broadbridge, 'Shipbuilding and the State in Japan since the 1950s', in *Modern Asian Studies,* Cambridge University Press, Vol. 11, Pt. 4, 1977, pp. 601-13.

Compared with the massive subsidies granted by the British Government to its shipbuilding industry during this period, the official help now given by the Japanese Government to its shipbuilders is small.[1] The comparison is also true of the other Japanese industries that have lately enjoyed the most conspicuous successes in foreign markets, notably motor cars, motor cycles and steel.

The different experience of those British and Japanese industries which have received large government subsidies since the war raises the question why government help to certain industries in Japan put them on the road to prosperity, whereas similar actions by British governments have been unsuccessful.[2]

Japanese economy and industry not monolithic or state run

Some Western writers,[3] with these and other examples of state intervention in mind, have designated the Japanese economy as monolithic and state run. But here they are in error. The relations between government and private industry in Japan are exceedingly complex and a foreigner is often baffled in trying to interpret what he observes. The influence of government policy on the course of development has been profound, but to emphasise the dominance of the state in economic affairs is to disregard two significant features of post-war Japan.

The first is the small size of the 'public' (government) sector by international standards: in the last decade the proportion of manpower employed in the 'public' sector (excluding the armed forces) was about 8 per cent in Japan compared with 22 per cent in the UK, while in the same period government expenditure in Japan as a percentage of GNP amounted to less than 20 per cent.

[1] 'Small' by international standards, that is. The Development Bank and the Export-Import Bank are the chief sources of the accommodation which takes the form of low-interest loans on exports for deferred payment. (Industrial Bank of Japan, *Japanese Finance and Industry,* October-December 1976.)

[2] A useful description of the various official schemes for assisting exports and overseas investments (including the several kinds of export credit insurance and tax concessions) is given in British Overseas Trade Board, *Japanese Government and Business,* London, 1974, pp. 26-32. The measures do not differ except in detail from those introduced by many other countries to assist exporters.

[3] Discussed in Boston Consulting Group, *Japan in 1980,* Financial Times, London, 1974, p. 22, and in W. W. Lockwood (ed.), *The State and Economic Enterprise in Japan,* Princeton University Press, Princeton, N.J., 1965, p. 503.

The second is that the overthrow of the militarist, authoritarian régime in 1945 released ebullient energies for private enterprise. The most progressive industrial firms since the war have been those founded by men coming from outside the ranks of the old Establishment. It is probable that the post-war government's chief contribution to economic progress was its provision of a congenial environment for innovators.

Any analysis of the distribution of economic initiative would be misleading if it led to the conclusion that the Japanese Government dictates policy to industry or, indeed, that all departments of the government speak with the same voice. Journalists have been especially misleading in writing of 'Japan Incorporated', for the truth is more intricate. The broad lines of strategy are normally discussed with the leaders of each industry by the civil servants of the Ministry of International Trade and Industry (MITI). What emerges, if the discussions are fruitful, is a 'consensus' which will influence the actions of individual firms. Whether government or industry holds the predominant power in these encounters is difficult to discover, and probably varies from industry to industry and from time to time.

The question has not been as important in post-war Japan as in other countries. What has made the co-operation between the two parties so effective has been the acceptance by both of rapid economic growth as a common over-riding purpose. This general agreement has cleared the way for unanimity on specific issues. But there has remained ample room for dissension about means. The intense competition and even bitter rivalries between firms or groups have on occasions impeded efforts to present a common front. Sometimes, government policy has been frustrated by the opposition of industrialists, or of particular firms.[1]

While the influence of the government in guiding the economy and the wide extent of co-operation between the state and industry can be conceded, Japanese industrial policy is not a seamless robe. The disasters that might befall the country if the government set out on a course of policy repugnant to private industry can be inferred from the post-war experience of Britain.

[1] An example of the former is the failure of the government's policy of industrial re-location in the early 1960s. An example of the latter is the Sumikin case of 1965-66. During a recession in the steel industry, MITI tried to bring about an agreed reduction of output, but one firm rejected the 'administrative guidance' and the scheme came to nothing.

IV. DISCOURAGEMENT OF IMPORTS?

A general recognition that direct subsidies and dumping are now of minor significance in explaining Japan's success in exports has diverted attention towards other factors that are said to have inhibited an equivalent increase in Western exports to Japan. The focus of these complaints is, particularly, her poor record as a customer for European manufactured goods. After 1972 critics could not direct their shafts at quantitative controls or high tariffs, for most of the former had been removed and the tariffs, in general, were moderate. Since liberalisation had not been accompanied by any substantial increase in the sales of foreign manufactures to Japan, the charge was now made that sales were impeded by 'administrative guidance', that is, the intricate web of regulations and administrative arrangements which cover imports into Japan (p. 49). The regulations include the specification of safety standards for such goods as pharmaceuticals and motor cars and also the legal and procedural difficulties imposed on importers.

Import controls liberalised, 1972

The import controls as they existed in the 1950s and 1960s left a good deal of discretion to the officials of MITI who were able to discriminate against competitive imports if they wished. It is likely that their decisions were at one time influenced by the state of Japan's balance of payments. But since 1972 the most important controls have been abolished so that the opportunities for administrative discrimination against imports have been, if not eliminated, at least much reduced.[1]

---

[1] The administration of import controls during the 1960s and early 1970s was carried out by a variety of measures:

   (i) The Automatic Application System (AA) which was equivalent to the British Open General Licence. This covered a wide variety of raw materials, semi-finished and manufactured goods which could be imported without restriction and for which import licences were issued automatically by the exchange banks.

   (ii) The Automatic Import Quota System (AIQ). Importers of goods covered by this system had to apply to MITI for foreign exchange certificates, valid

[Continued on page 32]

Other regulations still have the effect of making the lot of the importer harder than he thinks justified. Some of these regulations cover standards of quality and performance. They apply notably to motor cars where there are stringent specifications for safety and exhaust emissions, and also to tests imposed on pharmaceuticals and cosmetics. It is improbable that in the formulation of these standards the protection of domestic producers against foreign competition exerted any considerable influence. But it would be too much to expect that the problems they created for importers would have caused sleepless nights to the officials who drafted them.

It has been claimed by foreign traders and governments that, in drawing up these regulations, the Japanese have shown themselves indifferent to their international responsibilities and that they have made few attempts to co-ordinate them with the regulations of their trading partners. The Japanese Government has also been accused of altering these specifications abruptly, without any consultation with foreign governments or foreign importers.

Japan's insularity starts to crumble?

This self-regarding behaviour may be attributable to the concept the Japanese hold of themselves as a people somewhat aloof from the rest of the community of advanced trading countries, an attitude which the treatment of the Japanese by those countries has done nothing to modify.

During the last few years the Japanese Government, having realised that the export surpluses might provoke new restrictive measures in her chief markets, has gone far towards meeting these criticisms. It now accepts as valid, for example, the

[Continued from page 31]

for one month, which had to be exchanged for import licences at the foreign exchange banks. The application to MITI had to be accompanied by information about the goods and their prices. If the application was approved, subsequent applications for the same type of goods were granted automatically.

(iii) The Import Deposit System under which importers had to deposit cash with an exchange bank before the import.

(iv) The Standard Settlement System which subjected to official scrutiny import transactions that involved long-term deferred payment.

(v) Government Procurement. This provided for discrimination in favour of Japan-made goods in government purchases.

The AA System was superseded in 1972 by an Import Declaration System (which was unrestrictive), and all the other controls, except (iv), were abolished during the same year.

supplying countries' tests on pharmaceuticals, and it no longer insists that the goods should be re-tested in Japan.

The same is true for motor cars, where it has been agreed to send Japanese inspectors to Europe to carry out the necessary tests. Moreover, it has recently postponed for three years the application to foreign cars of the exhaust-emission standards that are to apply to Japanese cars in 1978. This action has been taken in the face of opposition from the environmental and consumer lobbies as well as from Japanese industrialists. The results have usually been achieved only after prolonged diplomatic pressure from Western governments.

Some of the other complaints can be dismissed as unreasonable. Importers are sometimes aggrieved because many of the regulations are available only in the Japanese language. Translations into European languages are often supplied, but the Japanese repudiate the suggestion that they should be obliged to provide such translations. They do not expect Western countries to supply *them* with Japanese translations of European or American import regulations.

Low tariffs but some high duties

A more serious objection is that while, in general, the Japanese tariffs are low, some of them are framed so as to throw an excessively heavy burden on importers. Scotch whisky is a case in point, as Japan is the second most important foreign market. Quota restrictions on whisky imports were removed in 1971, but very high taxes designed to protect the domestic industry remain; thus an import duty of 68 per cent *ad valorem* is imposed on Scotch whisky compared with a duty of only 28 per cent on Bourbon which is not competitive with any similar Japanese product.[1]

Another high protective duty that affects British goods is the 35-40 per cent duty on chocolate, biscuits and confectionery. These duties are supposed to compensate for the exceedingly high domestic prices for grain and sugar which are the consequence of the protection accorded to Japanese agriculture: e.g. the price of Japanese barley is three times the British price. The high protective duties on food do not seriously concern the British,[2] although they seriously impede the growth of

---

[1] The protective effect is all the more because the *ad valorem* liquor tax is imposed on imported whisky valued at c i.f. *plus* the import duty already paid.

[2] But, as already demonstrated, imports of Scotch whisky are heavily taxed.

exports from Australia and New Zealand, and to some extent from Continental countries. But Europe, in view of its own restrictionist agricultural policy, can hardly complain of similar discrimination by others, however objectionable it is in economic principle.

Finally, it is contended by some foreign firms that the Japanese trade mark laws afford them inadequate safeguards against rivals intent on infringing their rights. This law certainly presents features unfamiliar to Europeans, but the Japanese authorities have argued that, if foreigners take the trouble to accommodate themselves to its provisions, protection can be assured. In spite of this assurance, many foreign firms, with experience of the intricacies of the administrative system, are still unconvinced that the delays they suffer in securing registration may not be the result of design. The less the overt legal restrictions, the more the covert administrative ones.

Tardiness in relaxing outmoded restrictions

Although the Japanese authorities have been steadily modifying many of their administrative arrangements in response to diplomatic pressure from abroad, to some observers they seem to be inexcusably slow in abandoning practices or attitudes that were once appropriate to their economic condition, but are so no longer. In the past the peculiarities of Japanese consumption habits,[1] the consequence of long isolation from external influences, had proved useful to them in their struggle to maintain equilibrium in their balance of payments. These peculiarities enabled the authorities to press forward with a policy of rapid growth in the confident expectation that the rise in money incomes would not be followed by a corresponding rise in imports of consumption goods. It was safe for them to carry an expansionist policy further otherwise than would have been prudent. While Japan's international position was weak, this import inelasticity excited no adverse comment from outside.

The present conflict with her trading partners has arisen in part because of the persistence of this inelasticity into a period in which the competitive strength of her industries and the large size of her trading surplus have become two of the most

---

[1] In pre-war days many of the articles commonly consumed were peculiar to Japan: much of the food, clothing, domestic utensils and furnishings. Today most of them differ little from those in other developed countries.

conspicuous features of the international scene. What had its origin in inherited national consumption habits has been preserved not so much by deliberate intent as by an almost unconscious predilection for keeping trade at home.

It is easy to find examples of the continuation into the present of policies designed to deal with former problems. Thus, during the 1950s, when the balance of payments was always under threat, Japanese authorities and industrialists alike exerted themselves to save imports. This was achieved by modifying productive processes so as to reduce dependence upon imports of raw materials, or by displacing imports of finished goods by fostering home manufacture. The policy persisted, even after the motive for it had long disappeared; and, of course, it became easier to pursue as the technical efficiency of Japan's industry improved. In recent years Britain has built up a large market for agricultural tractors in Japan (to a value of £15·6 million in 1976), but this market is now being served in part by domestic producers. Three of the Japanese importers of foreign tractors have lately started to produce them, a transformation of customers into competitors that has been a familiar experience of British suppliers. It is not suggested that these tactics offend against any code of competition, only that they may be politically inexpedient at a time when Japan's success in international trade is provoking her trading partners to discriminate against her exports.

The more liberal policy pursued by Japan during the last few years has removed most of the factors once held responsible for her sweeping successes in export markets and for the failure of foreign manufacturers to obtain what they regard as a 'reasonable' share of her domestic market. Yet the imbalance in trade has continued and, since the 'oil shock' of 1973, the proportion of manufactures in her total imports has fallen steeply. So, many critics have changed their ground. Lack of success in selling to Japan is now widely attributed to the way in which her industrial and trading concerns are organised. This organisation, it is contended, is inimical to the enterprise of foreign competitors.

Distribution inefficient?

In the first place, it is asserted that Japan's distributive trade is inefficient by Western standards, resulting in excessively large mark-ups on the delivered prices of imported manufactures. Any price advantage commanded by a Western competitor is thus liable to be submerged by high distributive margins. Some impressive examples have been given. A man's suit which costs 50,000 yen f.o.b. (£110) retails in Japan for 200,000 to 250,000 yen, a cashmere pullover costing 1,115 yen f.o.b. sells for at least 4,000 yen, and Haig's Scotch Whisky, with a duty-free price of 8,500 yen a case, sells retail for 44,400 yen a case.[1] The most impressive example of all relates not to manufactures but to imported beef. A kilogram imported in January 1978 with an f.o.b. price of 498 yen and a c.i.f. price of 571 yen was sold retail for 2,408 yen.[2]

The reply commonly made by the Japanese is that the burden of high distribution costs has to be carried by their own manufacturers as well as by their foreign competitors. They admit that their way of trading has its peculiarities, but they argue that a foreign supplier must expect to adapt his methods to those that prevail in the market he hopes to serve, just as the Japanese themselves are obliged to make elaborate studies of foreign markets before they launch their overseas sales campaigns.

An exceptionally high proportion of Japanese consumer goods is sold through small unit shops, and the value of sales per employee is low by international standards. In 1970 there were 19 retail shops per 1,000 inhabitants in Japan, compared with 9 in the United States and 10 in Britain. These contrasts help to explain Japan's high distributive costs, but whether they 'prove' that the Japanese system is 'inefficient' is debatable. The Japanese may *prefer* to do their shopping in that way!

This answer goes some way towards meeting the complaint— but not the whole way. Foreign firms declare that their Japanese distributors tend to hold retail prices unchanged even when the import prices have been significantly reduced and that, in consequence, the penetration into the market even of goods apparently widely acceptable is impeded. A recent inquiry by the (Japanese) Economic Planning Board has produced evidence that supports this stricture, while a survey by MITI has shown

[1] The Mitsukoshi department store group is an important channel of distribution for high-quality British consumer goods. Many of these goods are bought direct by Mitsukoshi from the suppliers and thus escape the expense of sale through numerous intermediaries. Yet it is estimated that British goods bought by this firm for £10 million f.o.b. in 1977 will be sold retail for £29 million. (Department of Trade, *Trade and Industry*, HMSO, 11 November, 1977, p. 271.)

[2] *Japan Times Weekly*, 22 April, 1978.

that the prices of imported goods are high in Japan in comparison with those of the same imported goods in other countries. An imported American car with a c.i.f. price index of 1 has sold for 2·39 in Japan compared with 1·36 in West Germany. The distributive cost made up 46 per cent of the retail price in Japan compared with 8 per cent in Germany. For Scotch whisky (c.i.f. price 1) the disparity is between 8·68 in Japan and 2·58 in the United States.[1]

Structure of distributive trade and character of imported goods

Part of the explanation is to be found in the structure of the Japanese distributive trade and part in the character of a high proportion of the manufactured imports (p. 40). For most classes of finished manufactures the imports consist of high-quality products, or specialities, for which consumer demand is inelastic and competitive pressures weak.[2] The pride of the Japanese in their own products does not exclude a love of the novel and exotic, and some foreign goods enjoy a high prestige. But these are, *a fortiori*, expensive articles of distinction, the kind especially that satisfy the devotees of 'conspicuous waste'!

The advantage enjoyed by the foreign producer in 'luxury goods' does not extend to goods in mass demand, and in that category of imports he has continued to suffer handicaps. This feature of Japan's international trade is evident in motor cars. While her sales are mainly of vehicles that serve the mass market, her imports consist of high-quality cars. Thus there is a strong demand for Jaguars in Japan, indeed sales are limited chiefly by the capacity of Leylands to supply. But foreign competitors have made little headway in the lower-priced ranges. As we shall see presently, this failure has very little to do with import restrictions or with defects in the distributive system (pp. 44-46).

Japanese apologists have suggested that foreign firms have been technically incompetent in their methods of sale. They

---

[1] *Japan Times Weekly*, 19 November, 1977.

[2] The significance of competition in the pricing of imported goods is brought out by an inquiry conducted by the Economic Planning Agency. In the period from December 1976 to June 1977 the import prices of 15 of the items investigated went down, but in 9 of these cases the retail price went up. The EPA concluded that, as one might expect, it was only when competition was keen that the retail price followed the import price downwards. (*Japan Times Weekly*, 10 September, 1977.)

contend that the British practice of relying on sole agents (who may also be acting for Japanese firms) is unsatisfactory if a serious assault on a market is intended. In general, their criticisms are probably justified, although where the imports are speciality goods with a limited appeal, it may be too expensive for a firm to appoint its own representative to Japan, which is one of the alternatives proposed. Some Western firms have associated themselves with one or other of the large trading houses which dominate the commerce of Japan at home and abroad. Others have founded joint ventures for the distribution of their products (Leyland-Mitsui is a recent example), and these have often resulted in increased sales.[1]

Imports impeded by conglomerates?

A second criticism is more difficult to deal with. It is argued that the vertical organisation of the Japanese economy, where the interests of the large conglomerates extend to every sector, makes it difficult for European competitors to gain a foothold in the home market.[2] Even if the foreign competitors' prices are lower, preference in the choice of suppliers (of, say, engineering components) is (say the critics) usually given to other members of the same group. The same reluctance to order from abroad extends beyond the circle of the conglomerates. Japanese firms feel safer in favouring a supplier who is near at hand and whose methods of doing business they find congenial rather than a firm in a far-off country.

Discrimination for such reasons (which is not found only among Japanese firms) is not to be attributed entirely to national prejudice or fear of the unknown. The delivery of supplies from local producers is often more dependable than that from overseas, and a prospective buyer from abroad must balance that risk against price advantages. The charge of 'unfair' discrimination is attested by a few examples provided by British manufacturers who have been the victims. In some cases British firms have been asked to quote for orders already destined for a Japanese supplier simply with the object of beating down the latter's prices. In overseas contracts, the prices quoted by British manufacturers of components have

[1] But hampered in Leyland's case by its own self-imposed restrictions (footnote 1, p. 41.)

[2] The conglomerates are not monopolists but firms with widely ramifying interests. They often compete vigorously with one another.

been raised steeply by the Japanese main contractor before they were sent on to the customer; the object of this manoeuvre was presumably to ensure that a Japanese firm was allotted the order.

These are well authenticated complaints, but it is impossible to say how representative they are. It is doubtful whether the Japanese offend more grossly against the accepted code of commercial ethics than the nationals of other countries. The Americans, according to their competitors, discriminate in favour of home-produced aircraft. The British, so the French allege, discriminate in favour of their own producers of oil rigs. The British nationalised industries accord priority to British firms in their purchase of supplies. It is probable that this kind of discrimination, even if exceptional, is particularly dangerous to Japan at the time, since it strengthens the demand among her trading partners for restrictions on her trade.

There is the further argument that the integrated character of Japanese business creates ample opportunities for cross-subsidisation which may easily be manipulated so as to defeat foreign competition either in the home or the foreign markets. But cross-subsidisation prevails throughout the large-firm sector of industry in all countries (and not least in the national-ised part of British industry), and it is discreditable to treat Japan as if she were the only culprit. It is pertinent to point out that the 'public' sector, where discrimination for other than commercial reasons is likely to be especially widespread, is much smaller proportionately in Japan than in any Western country.[1]

In the end, one must recognise that the extent to which the abolition of formal restrictions opens up opportunities for free international competition rests in part on the existence of a community of trade practice. In Western countries there is sufficient mutual understanding of the non-official impediments to the freedom of trade that a would-be competitor is likely to encounter in the markets of those countries to enable him to judge what his own position will be. But Western firms in general have only a feeble grasp of Japan's social and business conventions, and where they are ignorant they are suspicious. The Japanese who trade in Western countries are the prey to similar perplexities; but they exert themselves more resolutely

[1] Above, p. 29.

CONSEQUENCES—

The importance of the argument for the reader and the British economy

1   MANKIND: Growth in production in any part of the world is likely to confer benefits, in increased income, on mankind as a whole. Japan's industrial advance, accompanied by a rise in her manufactured exports, should not be judged simply by its effects on the less efficient industries of her competitors.

2   BRITISH CONSUMERS: The growth in Japan's exports has given consumers in Britain and many other countries access to goods which some of them prefer to those from home or other sources. Restrictions on imports of manufactures from Japan would reduce British consumers' freedom of choice and their welfare.

3   BRITISH TAXPAYERS: The British public should not be required to provide lavish poor relief for those employed by Leyland and others and yet be deprived of the opportunity to buy the motor cars many prefer.

4   IMPORTERS AND DEALERS: The industrial and commercial development of Japan has produced reciprocal developments in other countries, including Britain. Importers of and dealers in Japanese manufactures have benefited from the growth in Japanese exports to Britain and other markets.

5 EXPORTERS: The rise in Japan's national income has increased her demand for imports, and British exporters have gained both from an expansion in their direct sales to Japan and also, indirectly, through the effect of Japan's growth on the incomes of overseas customers.

6 FINANCIAL AND SHIPPING SERVICES: The rise of Japan as an international trader has rapidly enlarged the demand for the financial and shipping services that Britain can provide. The increase in Japan's expenditure on these British services has gone far to offset the adverse balance on her commodity trade with Britain.

7 CONSEQUENCES FOR POLICY: The imbalance in Japan's commodity trade and the large surplus on her current trading account in recent years can be attributed mainly to her exceptionally high rate of industrial growth, just as Britain's chronic troubles with her balance of payments can be ascribed mainly to her comparatively low rate of growth.

8 The remedy must be sought not in erecting barriers to international trade (which would lead to economic stagnation) but in eliminating those that now exist (in Japan and elsewhere) and by reforms in the international monetary system and in domestic economic policies that will permit more rapid adjustments to changes in relative industrial efficiency.

9 When productive efficiency rises in a country (as in a firm), those who cannot match the improvement must be prepared to transfer their resources to other products, and government policies must be consistent with their so doing. Preserving the *status quo* in any part of economic life in the face of rapid technological and commercial change is a prescription for chronic unemployment and progressive impoverishment.

G.C.A.

than their European counterparts to reach an understanding of the oddities of their customers.

British successes in the Japanese market

From some of the complaints one might imagine that foreign firms had been decisively repelled in their efforts to secure a foothold in the Japanese market. A booklet issued by the British Overseas Trade Board in January 1976 dispels this conclusion by listing a series of British successes.[1] Thus, the British Oxygen Company (BOC) successfully sells medical equipment, welding products and high-vacuum equipment; Japan has become the best customer for one of the company's factories making welding equipment. BOC has maintained its own representative in Tokyo since 1968 and its joint ventures with Japanese firms have contributed to its marketing successes. British Engineers Ltd has done well in Japan with high-pressure valves, chassis for turntables and auto changers; Cadbury's with confectionery, despite the high duties; Davy International with gas plants and forging plants; EMI with brain scanners and radar tubes; Ercol with high-quality furniture; Foseco Minsep with chemical products and servicing equipment for the metallurgical industries; GKN, Glaxo, Judge, Massey Fergusson, Perkins Engines (diesel engines), Reid and Taylor (high-grade worsteds), Rolls-Royce (aero-engines), Gordon Russell, Stone Platt Industries (textile machinery and engineering components embodied in many Japanese exports) and, of course, the Scotch whisky distillers. Many of these firms use Japanese partners (including the big trading houses) to distribute their products. And a few have established joint ventures for distribution, assembly and even manufacture.

In discussing their experience, a number of the firms emphasised that success depends on understanding the nature of the Japanese market and distributive system (which 'are like unto no other'),[2] and that understanding can be reached only by patience and attention to detail, qualities which the Japanese themselves certainly display in their own ventures overseas. These examples serve, however, to demonstrate a distinctive feature of the import trade in manufactures, namely that the British successes have been largely confined to specialities and high-quality goods. Mass-produced articles are notably absent

[1] British Overseas Trade Board, *British Successes in Japan*, London, January 1976.
[2] The words of one of the successful exporters to Japan.

[40]

from the list, as they are from a wide range of Western products sold in Japan.[1]

It is an important question whether the explanation is to be found in the classical theory of comparative advantage—that Japan's factor endowment is such that it is rational for her to concentrate her manufacturing resources on mass-produced goods and to import specialities.[2]

Comparative advantage—the classical doctrine

At one time an appeal to the classical theory of international trade would have been heeded by governments in this country, even if their actions were sometimes inconsistent with it. The classical theory asserted, in effect, that trade among countries was determined by their comparative advantages in various lines of production, and that interference with the market mechanism through which the reciprocal flow of goods and services was determined would diminish the incomes of the trading partners. Adam Smith put it very simply:

> 'If a foreign country can supply us with a commodity cheaper than we ourselves can make it, better buy it of them with some part of the produce of our own industry, employed in a way in which we have some advantage.'

Modern governments, however, find it difficult to accept this common-sense doctrine. They are persuaded that, in a world subject to rapid economic change, they are often justified (in the interest of full employment or the balance of payments) in introducing measures to protect domestic industries against foreign competition or to strengthen their country's exporting capacity. These policies have not lacked defenders among economists.

It is true that an increase in foreign competition may well be to the detriment of a country, if the competition occurs in classes of goods which it was previously well fitted to produce.

---

[1] There are exceptions, such as Coca-Cola. Moreover, the failure of Westerners to make headway in the mass markets is not necessarily always the fault of the Japanese. Mitsui, Leyland's partner, wanted to try to sell the cheaper cars in Japan, but Leyland preferred to concentrate on 'prestige' models. (J. Corbett, *The European Community's Trade with Japan*, Australian National University, Canberra, 1978, p. 54.)

[2] Other information about British export successes and also joint ventures between British and Japanese firms in Japan and in third countries is given in Japan Information Centre, *British Trade with Japan*, London, 1977, pp. 24-5.

But the exclusion of such goods from the home market by protection or quotas will almost certainly make matters *worse*, immediately by depriving consumers of the benefit of cheaper imports, in the long run by tying resources to forms of production for which the former comparative advantages have been lost, and in a broader sense by stimulating trade restrictions throughout the world.

People (including some economists) who favour import restrictions in these circumstances seem to assume that, unless the threatened industries are protected, the resources displaced from them will be unable to find employment elsewhere in the home economy. This result would, of course, follow if resources were completely immobile, if the wage terms on which the displaced workers would accept employment in another industry were out of accord with their productivity in that employment, or if industrial enterprise in the country had withered away. As applied to Britain today, despite her present economic weaknesses, such a degree of pessimism is unjustified.

In any event, the causes that give rise to the pessimism cannot be removed by policies that increase structural rigidity: they would only hasten a decline. A solution must be found in the elimination of the monopolistic and trade union rigidities by institutional reforms and the restoration of an economic and political environment favourable to enterprise.

V. A VERDICT

The discussion has turned on various explanations of Japan's massive export surplus, as did the increased imbalances in her trade with European countries and the United States in particular. The failure of Western manufacturers to gain what they regard as a reasonable share of her home market has also been analysed. The popular view finds the chief explanation in 'unfair' business methods such as dumping and subsidies to promote exports and restrictions and discrimination to protect the Japanese home market.

There can be no doubt that in the first two decades after the war Japan was guilty as accused. Nor can one deny that, even after Japan's international position had improved, the dismantling of the controls, especially over imports, was exceedingly slow. Since 1970, however, liberalisation has proceeded apace. Subsidies and quantitative import controls have not been entirely abandoned, but Japan now makes no more use of these devices than Western countries, including Britain.[1]

Japan's import duties not out of line with Europe or US

In general, Japan's level of import duties on manufactures, moreover, compares favourably with those of European countries and the United States, especially since the unilateral reduction of her duties in 1972.[2] 'Administrative guidance' of a kind adverse to foreign competition in the home market had at one time a powerful influence on trade, but it has yielded to diplomatic pressure from abroad. It is now used largely to persuade Japanese exporters whose successes have seriously

---

[1] The Under-Secretary of State for the Department of Industry stated, on 7 March, 1977, that the British Government during the previous three years had injected over £6,000 million into manufacturing industry, apart from another £2,500 million paid in support of the nationalised industries, industrial training, redundancy payments and labour market services. (Quoted by Professor John Jewkes in *Delusions of Dominance*, Hobart Paper 76, IEA, 1977, pp. 58-9.) In restrictions on imports, Britain today is probably a worse offender than Japan.

[2] Another unilateral reduction in the Japanese import duties is promised for the Spring of 1978, in advance of the conclusion of the present multilateral trade negotiations.

[43]

threatened the prosperity of some Western industries to moderate their 'attack' on foreign markets. So one can conclude that, in recent years, the so-called 'unfair' methods of competition, including 'administrative guidance', have had only a marginal effect and that their effect has been steadily weakened.

Whether the vertical organisation of the economy and the prevalence of cohesive groups in industry are still responsible for discrimination remains obscure. An outsider has no means of discovering the extent to which cross-subsidisation in the large diversified firms affects the pricing of particular products. Again, many Japanese firms prefer, *ceteris paribus*, to direct their orders to domestic suppliers; this preference for keeping the trade at home may possibly be stronger than in Europe where there is a closer community of interest and commercial practice. Yet, despite the high degree of integration in Japanese business, one cannot be certain that this is now so. The West can produce plenty of examples of discrimination in favour of domestic suppliers, especially in the nationalised industries.

Distributive system helps domestic over foreign suppliers

It is probable that Japan's complex distributive system affords advantages to her own over foreign suppliers to the home market for consumer goods. Where the handicap is the result of the unfamiliarity of foreigners with Japanese ways, it can be offset, as some successful Western firms have shown, by a thorough study of local conditions. The undoubted 'stickiness' of the retail prices charged for some Western imports can be attributed mainly to the character of the imported products and, in the market for specialities, to the absence of competition for which the foreign suppliers themselves may be partly responsible because of the channels of distribution they use.

Japan's industrial efficiency the chief factor

All these factors are now of secondary importance in explaining both Japan's position as an international competitor in the market for manufactured goods and her continuing surplus on current account. *The chief reason is the rise in her industrial efficiency relative to that of other countries during the last 20 years.*

The improvement was based on heavy investment in high-technology industries and on the transfer of manpower on an enormous scale from low-productivity to high-productivity industries. It was initiated by forceful entrepreneurs operating in an economic and political environment congenial to their talents. It was sustained by a body of highly trained managers and technicians and by a system of industrial relations well attuned to the requirements of an advanced industrial society.[1] The comparative figures for productivity and the trend of relative export prices in recent years confirm this explanation of Japan's success as an international trader (Tables IV and V, p. 55).

Economic growth and export strength

The improvement in Japan's competitive strength in export markets was a by-product of her high rate of economic growth, itself caused by increases in industrial productivity. Contrary to what is often asserted, her economic growth was not export-led, although in periods of recession (such as the present) her structural flexibility has enabled firms to shift their production quickly from the home to the export market and so to maintain aggregate demand. Apart from these short-term fluctuations, exports as a ratio to GNP have remained almost constant for the last 15 years at about 10 per cent.[2] Their steep absolute increase in value has been a concomitant of the country's rapid economic growth.

The principle of high growth as an over-riding national purpose has had a marked effect on the pricing policy of Japanese companies. In the pursuit of growth, and in the knowledge that they have been working with the grain of a generally approved design, firms have been ready to accept low profit margins in the confident expectation that a high turnover would follow. Such a policy, as Japan's experience shows, can yield particularly striking results in the capital-intensive industries, on which the country's development has been concentrated in the last quarter of a century. The advantage it gives to Japan in international competition needs no emphasis.

Japan's investment is mainly in the hands of private institutions and their choice of industries for investment has had a close bearing on her rate of growth and advance as an international competitor. Steel, ships, electronic goods and motor

---

[1] [Explanations of these assertions, and an account of 'Ringisho' and the Japanese system of industrial relations, can be found in Chiaki Nishiyama, G. C. Allen, *The Price of Prosperity: Lessons from Japan*, Hobart Paper 58, IEA, 1974.—ED.]

[2] The ratio has risen to about 12 per cent during the present recession.

cars were all products for which foreign and domestic demand increased exceptionally in the 20 years before the present recession. Demand for these goods was elastic, especially for the varieties on which Japan concentrated her efforts. Between 1953 and 1970, the rise in her relative industrial efficiency allowed her to reduce export prices by some 20 per cent, compared with the export prices of her chief competitors. She was able, as a result, to capture a high proportion of the world's growing demand for industrial goods.

The competitive superiority was carried into the 1970s. Between 1970 and 1976 output per man-hour in Japan's manufacturing industry continued to increase relative to that of other nations. This improvement in productivity has lately been offset in part by the more rapid rise in wages, compared with those of her competitors. The exceptionally fast expansion in her exports during the last two years, despite this check to her comparative advantages, can be ascribed largely to the more general recognition of the high quality of her industrial products and to the growing efficiency of her merchanting organisations overseas. But one cannot rule out the possibility that government policy, exerted in the main through the banking system, has affected the actions of traders from time to time or that cross-subsidisation within the big conglomerates still makes a contribution, though a minor one, to the success of the export drive.

Under-valuation of the yen

As in the 1930s, the exceedingly rapid growth of exports during the last 15 years has been attributed to the under-valuation of the yen. In the early and middle 1930s, the steep fall in the exchange rate was accompanied by a worsening in the terms of trade and a decline in the living standards of many Japanese workers. In contrast, the under-valuation of the last 15 years occurred because the rate of exchange between the yen and other currencies remained stable (except for temporary fluctuations), while costs and prices in Japan were falling relatively to those of her trading partners.[1] So the factoral terms of trade[2] moved decisively in her favour. Japan dealt with her

[1] The 'Nixon shock' of 1971 led, of course, to the rise in the price of yen in terms of dollars.

[2] In other words, because of the increase in her relative productivity, she was able to obtain a given quantity of imports with a decreasing outlay of real resources.

[46]

favourable balance on current account partly by increasing her foreign investment and partly by accumulating large reserves of gold and foreign exchange.

During the last decade favourable current balances have enabled the Japanese to make substantial investments abroad in manufacturing undertakings. It might have been supposed that Britain, where some Japanese firms have established factories, would have welcomed without reservation any foreign enterprise and investment which might help to redress her industrial inferiority. But the hostile reception given by vested interests to Hitachi's proposal to build an assembly factory for television sets on the North-East coast shows otherwise.

In the light of this obstruction and other similar experiences, the Japanese may be forgiven for supposing that Britain's indignation about Japan's imbalance is spurious, since she has rejected one of the most obvious remedies.

The growth in the reserves was checked by the 'oil shock' and fell steeply after 1973, but since 1975 they have risen rapidly as the monetary authorities bought dollars on a large scale to keep down the exchange rate. From the beginning of 1977, in response to pressure from other countries, the Bank of Japan has allowed the exchange value of the yen to float, and between January and November its appreciation in terms of dollars was about 23 per cent. (By the Spring of 1978 the appreciation had amounted to about 27 per cent.)

It can be argued that this appreciation was overdue and that, if the yen had been permitted to rise earlier, the imbalance would not have become so large. In the long run such a policy would have brought a solution, but in the short run the rise in the yen may well enlarge Japan's surplus on current account. Export earnings are not likely to be quickly affected, while the inelasticity of the demand for the country's imports in response to price changes will reduce almost immediately the total payments due.[1]

The Japanese authorities, of course, have not been influenced by these considerations, but their reluctance to permit a large

[1] Japan's system of industrial relations may influence the response of exports to the rising yen. Since firms are committed to the 'lifelong employment' of their established workers, they have a strong inducement to maintain production even if this means lowering prices and accepting some losses on export sales, especially at times when domestic demand is depressed.

appreciation of the yen once the present recession began is readily comprehensible. During the last two years exports have been the one strong factor in aggregate demand. Consumer expenditure has been held down by the smallness of the increases secured by the workers in the last two Spring 'Wage Offensives'; private investment in equipment, which in the past supplied the main impulse to growth, has been depressed; and the rise in public expenditure has been quite insufficient to fill the gap. To damage Japan's competitive strength in foreign markets would be to remove what is at present the chief prop to the economy.

Is Japan's competitive strength insecure?

Many critics will not be impressed by this argument. They have observed that, even during the period of mounting prosperity, the Japanese authorities were equally resolute in their determination to keep the exchange rate from rising. An explanation of their reluctance has been suggested (p. 12), namely their scepticism about the permanence of the conditions upon which Japan's competitive strength has been based. Foreigners who fasten their eyes on Japan's present huge surplus forget that for the first 25 years after the war her recovery and expansion were constantly under threat from the precarious state of her balance of payments. This weakness had its source in the failure of her export trade to keep pace with her industrial growth. It is only within the last 10 years that she has earned a substantial surplus on her current account. Even in that period, as a result of the sudden rise in oil prices, her account for two years showed a large deficit. The Japanese are less likely than their critics to fall victims to the fallacy of the constant trend, i.e., the commonly held presumption that a trend, once established, will continue indefinitely! They are aware that a change from surplus to deficit may occur unpredictably and suddenly in a world of rapid technical progress, capricious markets and political instability. They do not regard their future as assured.

With the well-attested worthlessness of long-term economic forecasts in mind, it is not prudent to speculate on the course of Japan's trade and payments during the next decade. Such inhibitions will not deter others, but one can be reasonably confident that Clio, from the comfortable distance of the late

1980s, will find ample cause for making her usual ironical comment on their prophecies.[1]

Economic (and political) effects of 'administrative guidance'

In the meantime, the interests of the Japanese, or so it seems to an outside observer, lie in getting rid of any residual practices that give the least excuse for discriminating against her own exports. She would almost certainly be one of the chief sufferers from any reversal of the post-war trend towards trade liberalisation to which the present disorder in international finance offers a threat. Her government, if not the whole of her business community, is aware of the danger. During the course of 1977 it affirmed on several occasions its commitment to a policy of limiting the growth of exports damaging to domestic producers overseas and of encouraging imports of manufactured goods. It hopes to limit exports by persuasion and 'administrative guidance',[2] a policy which may sometimes be justified by political expediency, but is economically pernicious since it is restrictive of international trade and harmful to foreign consumers of Japanese products.

I refer here to the expediency of fobbing off discrimination threatened by foreign governments against Japanese goods; 'voluntary' restrictions on exports of certain goods are among the devices employed. In this connection, however, the Japanese Government is faced with an internal political problem as well as an international problem. The Liberal-Democratic Government, which has held office since the Second World War (but for one brief interval), has been closely allied with business interests and has followed an economic policy which they have favoured. The policy has been that of giving priority to economic, especially industrial, growth. The conspicuous rise in the standard of life that has attended the

---

[1] E. W. Streissler, *Pitfalls in Econometric Forecasting*, Research Monograph 23, IEA, 1970; George Polanyi, *Short-term Forecasting: A Case Study*, Background Memorandum 4, IEA, 1973; James B. Ramsey, *Economic Forecasting—Models or Markets?*, Hobart Paper 74, IEA, 1977.

[2] Foreigners are inclined to make too much of the susceptibility of Japanese business to 'administrative guidance' which, from some of their observations, one might suppose to be quite unknown to the West. On the contrary, since the war the British Government has relied increasingly on 'administrative guidance' to achieve its aims. It was used, for instance, to coerce, or persuade, motor firms in the early 1960s to locate new capacity in areas of official choice. 'Extra-legal pressure', 'jollying along' has become a familiar feature of British government. As is well known, 'administrative guidance' has exerted a particularly strong, and usually perverse, influence on the decisions of the boards of the nationalised industries.

[49]

policy has won for it popular support which has continued despite the present recession. The Government's position would be jeopardised if it lost the support of the business community, or if the general standard of life ceased to rise. Its policies are framed with those dangers in mind.

In other words, it must be hesitant in its response to foreign diplomatic pressure if, in responding, it might seriously antagonise the business community. Some observers may think that, in view of its vulnerable position, it has been bold in its measures of liberalisation. There are also cross-currents. For example, the party in power since the war has also derived much support from the rural community. So the high protection given to farmers is explained largely by its concern with the rural vote; it may be influenced also by the once widely prevalent sentiment that finds in the agricultural life a repository of old values in a time of social disintegration.

Policies and problems for the Japanese economy

The encouragement of imports as a means of reducing the imbalance calls for the abolition of the surviving trade and exchange restrictions, the simplification of import regulations and, despite the qualifications already mentioned, a freely floating exchange rate. All these are eminently desirable. But, as the analysis in this *Paper* shows, such policies *in the short run* would make only a modest contribution to the solution of the problem, which has its roots in the disparity between Japan's rate of growth and that of other industrial nations during the last two decades.

This disparity has accompanied her relatively rapid advance in productivity over an ever-widening range of industries and is not likely to contract until she has deployed her resources. Higher personal incomes and the direction of a larger proportion of her investment (public and private) into amenities, housing and welfare at the expense of investment in industrial equipment, are the directions in which solutions may be found.[1]

[1] A recently issued White Paper on welfare has instituted comparisons between Japan and other countries in provisions for welfare. It shows that, although Japan's expenditure on social security rose from 9·2 per cent of the national income to 11 per cent between 1975 and 1977 (fiscal years), this proportion is low compared with that of Sweden (30 per cent), West Germany, France and Italy (20 per cent), and Britain and the United States (15 per cent). The significance of these figures is rather uncertain because of differences in the age distribution in the various countries as well as in social organisations (e.g. the acceptance or otherwise by families of obligations to the old and ill). (*Japan Times Weekly*, 10 December, 1977.) Japan's housing standards have not kept pace with her advance in manufacturing industry.

This change has been approved in principle by the Japanese Government, but so far the structural adjustments have not been conspicuous. Investment in the government sector has certainly been much increased, but a large share of the additional funds has been applied to improving the part of the infrastructure that serves manufacturing industry (e.g. transport) rather than to the provision of welfare.

If the new policy were pressed home, the Japanese export industries would probably lose some of their competitive superiority and the opportunities for foreign suppliers to the home market might be enlarged. But it is not easy for the Japanese authorities to deviate from a course which they have pursued with outstanding success for over a quarter of a century. Their anxieties are all the stronger because they are being called upon to take such momentous decisions in a period of domestic recession. Nevertheless, without structural adjustment in the economy, it is improbable that the problem of the imbalance can be solved or that the 'threat' to the international order which it now poses can be lifted.

One consideration remains. The last word in this controversy must be spoken by, or on behalf of, the consumers, the Forgotten People in the contentions of governments and industrial interests. Japan's goods have not been forced upon reluctant buyers. Her cars, radios, television sets and ships have been outstandingly successful in international competition because, for reasons of price and quality, consumers have often found them more acceptable than the products of other countries. In a word, it is the consumers who have been the chief beneficiaries of Japan's industrial efficiency and her enterprise in foreign markets. It is they who would suffer most from further restrictions on the sale of the goods for which they have unmistakably shown their preference. This is as relevant *mutatis mutandis* to the right of Japanese consumers to freedom of choice as to that of Europeans and Americans.

Should Britain impose import controls on Japanese goods?
The increase in Japan's exports to Britain and Continental Europe has provoked some Western manufacturers damaged by her competition to demand further import controls. Although so far the British Government has resisted these demands, Ministers have sometimes spoken as if the protests

[51]

from the vested interests were justified.[1] The almost hysterical comments of some politicians and journalists on Japanese commercial enterprise in Europe are all the more remarkable when we reflect that imports from Japan in recent years have made up less than 3 per cent of Britain's total imports and about 4 per cent of the imports of the EEC.

It is true that the competition has been concentrated on a rather narrow range of products, e.g., motor vehicles, electronic goods and steel. The British have emphasised particularly the damage caused by Japanese imports to the home motor industry. Yet, as already shown (p. 26), the decline in the share of the home market now in the hands of British manufacturers has been brought about mainly by the advance in the imports of German, French and Italian vehicles; Japan's share has amounted to only about 10 per cent.

The quantitative importance of Japanese products in the British market is thus low. To restrict their entry further would have only a small direct effect on output and employment in Britain, while it would deprive consumers of products on which some of them set high store. The *indirect* effects of a restrictive policy might be harmful to British industry. Even if the Japanese Government was not provoked into retaliatory action, it would certainly bring to an end its present efforts to smooth the path of the British exporter to Japan. Moreover, the Japanese manufacturing capacity now being used to supply goods for sale in Britain would probably be diverted to serving other markets where they might displace British exports.

In the past British and other Western manufacturers have made justifiable complaints about Japan's own import controls and subsidies to domestic producers, but these controls and subsidies have now been largely removed. Indeed, Japan relies far less on subsidies to sustain her industries than Britain. The reasons why British and other Western firms have been comparatively unsuccessful in selling manufactures to Japan are complicated, but one is undoubtedly that few of them have displayed the same resolute enterprise in their export drives as the Japanese have shown in *their* commercial ventures overseas. In any event, there is little sense in making much of bilateral trade or current account surpluses or deficits. It is Japan's huge current *global* surpluses during 1976 and 1977 that have been

[1] Speech by the Secretary of State for Trade to the International Press Club, Tokyo, 8 April, 1974.

a reasonable cause for anxiety. They have been brought about, as has been shown, chiefly by the increase in Japan's relative industrial efficiency; even the steep rise in the yen in 1977-78 has not yet closed the gap between her costs and those of her competitors. The world's monetary system has found it exceptionally difficult to handle the financial problem so caused, partly because of the suspicion with which Japanese investment overseas is viewed in some quarters. For example, South-East Asian countries seem an obvious host for Japanese enterprise, but the growth of her industrial investment in these countries has been condemned by nationalists as 'economic imperialism'. The rejection by the British of a proposed Japanese investment in an electronics plant shows that this attitude is not confined to the under-developed countries (p. 47).

As history testifies, whenever a country outstrips others in industrial productivity, problems of adjustment are bound to appear. The rise in Japan's efficiency in manufacturing has faced not only Britain with costs of adjustment, but also Japan herself. There, certain industries such as textiles, which cannot match the high-technology industries in performance, are in retreat. But a readiness to accept a continuous re-allocation of resources has been, and remains, a condition of material progress. It would be nonsensical if the experience of the last two years (which may prove abnormal) prompted British or European governments to embrace policies damaging to the system of multilateral trade that has been fostered since the Second World War.

STATISTICAL APPENDIX

TABLE I

JAPAN'S BALANCE OF PAYMENTS, 1968 TO 1977

(*US $million*)

Calendar Year	Exports	Imports	Trade Balance	Services	Current Balance*
1968	12,751	10,222	2,529	−1,306	1,048
1969	15,679	11,980	3,699	−1,399	2,119
1970	18,969	15,006	3,963	−1,785	1,970
1971	23,566	15,779	7,787	−1,738	5,797
1972	28,032	19,061	8,971	−1,883	6,624
1973	36,264	32,576	3,688	−3,510	−136
1974	54,480	53,044	1,436	−5,842	−4,693
1975	54,734	49,706	5,028	−5,354	−682
1976	66,026	56,139	9,887	−5,867	3,680
1977	79,300	61,810	17,490	−6,059	11,045

*Including transfers. Exports f.o.b., imports c.i.f..

TABLE II

JAPAN'S TRADE WITH EUROPE AND UK, 1968 TO 1977

(*US $million*)

Year	Exports to Europe	Imports from Europe	Trade Balance*	Exports to UK	Imports from UK	Trade Balance
1968	1,896	1,878	18	365	257	108
1969	2,407	2,067	340	348	330	18
1970	3,363	2,555	808	480	395	85
1971	3,945	2,641	1,304	574	417	157
1972	5,504	3,172	2,332	979	501	478
1973	7,377	5,297	2,080	1,357	761	596
1974	10,276	6,930	3,346	1,530	878	652
1975	10,346	5,778	4,568	1,473	810	663
1976	13,777	6,320	7,457	1,400	843	557
1977	15,758	7,206	8,552	1,950	959	991

* Including the USSR for which the balance in 1976 was about US $1,000 million and in 1977 about US $500 million in Japan's favour.

TABLE III

JAPAN'S EXPORTS TO EUROPE AS A PROPORTION OF HER TOTAL EXPORTS,* SELECTED YEARS, 1960 TO 1977

	%
1960	12
1967	14
1970	15
1976	17
1977	18

*Excluding USSR.

TABLE IV

COMPARATIVE OUTPUT PER MAN-HOUR IN MANUFACTURING, 1970 TO 1976

1970=100

	US	W. Germany	France	UK	Japan
1972	110	111	114	112	114
1974	116	122	126	118	136
1975	118	126	120	118	131
1976	124	135	134	123	148

TABLE V

EXPORT AND IMPORT PRICE INDICES, 1966 TO 1977
(*Japanese Ministry of Finance*)
1970=100

	Export Prices	Import Prices
1966	88	96
1967	91	96
1968	91	95
1969	95	95
1970	100	100
1971	100	102
1972	99	94
1973	107	106
1974	148	188
1975	148	205
1976	144	207
1977	153	200

A Japanese Commentary

by

YUKIHIDE OKANO

Professor of Economics, University of Tokyo

1. *Introduction*

Professor G. C. Allen is admirably correct and fair-minded in his analysis of Japan's trading practices. Though he is well-known in Japan as an expert on the Japanese economy, those Japanese who do not know him will be very surprised by his thorough understanding of the Japanese economy.

My broad conclusions are very similar to Professor Allen's. My comments and suggestions are based on my observations as an economist, experiences as a consumer and discussions with Japanese manufacturers, bankers and civil servants.

The Japanese 'irritant'

What is the central issue? What irritates Western countries: the huge surpluses in Japan's balance of trade or the expansion of her exports to Western countries? It is true that Japan's trade advance has been, for the Western world as a whole, the more damaging to domestic manufacturers because it has been concentrated on a rather narrow front and is 'horizontal' (pp. 14-15). Would Western countries be satisfied if Japan's trade surpluses decreased whatever measures she might take? Probably not. What Western countries want seems to me to be that Japan's imbalance of trade should be corrected under the present 'horizontal' structure of trade between the West and Japan. But reducing Japan's huge trade surpluses is only part of the problem: a decrease in her surpluses would not necessarily improve the balance of payments and employment of Western countries.

The solution, from the viewpoint of Western countries, might be an increase either in their (direct) exports to Japan or in their exports to non-Western countries which have surpluses on their trade with Japan.

Thus, Japan's pattern of trade with the rest of the world is of substantial significance to Western countries.

2. 'Dumping'

(i) 'Social dumping'

During the 1930s, after Japan abandoned the gold standard, her exports made remarkable advances in spite of the decrease in world trade and deterioration of the terms of trade. This phenomenon was called 'social dumping'. I myself refrain from commenting on whether it really was so. But Professor R. Komiya has argued that it was neither appropriate nor reasonable to call it 'social dumping' in a derogatory sense. That wages were low in comparison with Western countries was simply a result of low marginal productivity of labour, and it should be noted that trade was almost balanced in the 1930s. Japan's foreign exchange policy can hardly be regarded as a 'beggar-my-neighbour policy' based on devaluation of the yen.[1] Many economists, particularly Marxian ones, nevertheless regard it as 'social dumping' in a derogatory sense.

(ii) Sporadic dumping

Professor Allen observes that the periods of domestic recession in Japan have been associated with a sharp rise in exports by volume, though not necessarily by value. But this association may be, though to a much smaller degree than in the 1960s, attributed to the financial structure of Japanese industry. Excepting those firms which recently went bankrupt, like Eidai, or those that have fallen into heavy debt, like Fuji Sash and its subsidiary company, quite a few, including widely-known Japanese firms, have not been dependent upon bank loans to finance expansion and inventory investment.[2] And the rise in exports during recessions might be attributed to Japanese firms adapting themselves to changing circumstances rather than to sporadic dumping.

Wages, moreover, are to some degree flexible if bonuses are taken into account. In recessions, firms at first reduce bonus payments, in spite of laying off workmen, with no reduction in

[1] Ryutaro Komiya and Akihiro Amano, *International Economics*, Iwanami Shoten, 1972, pp. 120-1.

[2] That the rate of inventory liquidation in the period of recession has been considerably lower in the 1970s than in the 1950s and 1960s might be explained, at least partly, by lessened dependence of firms upon bank loans.

[58]

regular wages.[1] Thus, the cost of labour per unit of production might be lower in recessions than during booms. Consequently, in recessions firms might be able to export their products at to some extent *lower* prices than during booms without decreasing employment and production.

It is in practice hard to judge whether a producer is engaged in dumping or not, because it depends on the prices in the domestic market compared with export prices. In the steel industry, for instance, there are at least two categories of prices: the long-term contract price, applied to automobile manufacturers and so forth, and the (usually higher) price in the spot market. Export prices are likely to be between the two.

3. The influence of government policy

Professor Allen's views on the influence of government policy on the course of development and the effect of 'administrative guidance' on Japanese business accord with mine, though many Japanese economists, and more especially civil servants, tend to overrate their role and effect. The influence of government policy on development has been marginal. The Japanese Government has established 'economic planning' programmes several times to assist development. Though often misunderstood as centralised economic planning similar to that in socialist states, Japanese 'planning' is no more than economic projection. If a series of economic projections had any influence on Japan's economic growth, it would be because Japanese firms became confident of the prospects for economic growth and of government policy towards it.

The effects of 'administrative guidance'

'Administrative guidance' seems to have been effective only when the administrative authorities could bring profit to firms through it. Otherwise, at least some firms would not follow it.

---

[1] One of the reasons why Japan has been able to keep 'life-time' employment might be this flexibility of wages. Table 1 (p. 70) shows that, allowing for inflation, regular wages and salaries in manufacturing industry on average rose by between 10 and 20 per cent per annum during the period 1973-76—and in 1974 by 26 per cent. But bonuses rose by only 1·1 per cent in 1975 and 11·0 per cent in 1976 compared with 36·1 per cent in 1973 and 31·4 per cent in 1974. In 1975 *real* wages and salaries indeed fell by 0·5 per cent compared with 1974. When depression persists, firms are obliged to restrict their employment, particularly in chronically depressed industries.

'Administrative guidance' by MITI was effective only when it was associated with powers which could be used discriminatively against firms that did not follow the guidance. In the oil refining industry, for example, firms were once under the control of MITI through the quota system for imported crude oil. They were obliged to follow the guidance. Even so, MITI sometimes faced difficulties in dissuading firms from expanding their refinery capacity.[1]

'Administrative guidance' is effective to the extent that it leads firms to reach a 'consensus' which will influence the actions of individual firms in an industry. 'Administrative guidance' is probably effective in shortening the time required to achieve 'consensus' where it would have been achieved in any event. The guidance would hardly be effective if 'consensus' would never have been attained because of serious conflicts among firms.[2]

Generally speaking, as Professor Allen has said, Japanese industries are very competitive in spite of the desire of MITI to keep firms under its control and of the desire of some firms to cartelise their industries. And it is due to keen competition that Japanese firms have hitherto achieved efficient production and technological innovation in some manufacturing industries, notably in automobiles and electronics.[3]

4. *Regulations on standards of quality and performance*

These regulations have been regarded as non-tariff barriers against imports. Whether or not any of them were specifically designed to restrict imports, it seems that most were imposed reluctantly by the government under pressure from consumer campaigns backed by newspapers. The most striking example was the control of motor-car exhaust emissions.

The stringent specifications for motor cars were not imposed with the intention of restricting imports. Under strong pressure

---

[1] It is ironical that MITI's policy gave the firms an incentive to *expand* their refinery capacity, since the allotment of crude oil among them was based on each firm's production of refined oil and its capacity. The same situation was observed in the sugar refining industry which has long suffered from excess capacity.

[2] In 1977 MITI urged the establishment of a specific kind of anti-depression cartel for steel bars which could penalise outsiders by law. But one company outside the cartel, Tokyo Seitetsu, the most efficient in the industry, which had always been an outsider, took legal proceedings against it.

[3] Japanese motor-car production after the war began in the early 1950s with the importation of technology from British and French car manufacturers.

from the anti-motoring and 'environmentalist' lobbies, the government was obliged to impose more stringent exhaust emission specifications than it had expected. It did so simply because the US Government had passed the Clean Air Act of 1970. The Japanese Government could not do other than adopt specifications as stringent as those of the US (the most stringent at that time) in order to show its serious concern over pollution. Japanese car makers complained that no technology was available to meet the new specifications, the most stringent in the world. All the car makers spent a considerable amount of money on research and development. By successfully maintaining the efficiency of fuel consumption, which had been expected to drop with the amount of pollutant in exhaust emissions, they maintained the competitiveness of Japanese cars in export markets.

The government has been more and more pressed by the public to take responsibility for safety standards, public health and the protection of the environment. It has therefore been obliged to extend and strengthen its regulations, which now constitute a kind of non-tariff barrier unfavourable to Western exports to Japan. Perhaps, however, the government and manufacturers should not really be blamed for discrimination against foreign exporters resulting from safety and environmental regulations.

5. The 'peculiarities' of Japanese consumption habits

Are Japanese consumption habits really peculiar? During the period when the balance of payments was under threat (i.e. until the late 1960s), the government encouraged consumers to buy home-produced goods. Yet Japanese consumers had a thirst for imported goods and the government therefore tried to restrict imports by various means, such as high import duties, import licensing and quotas. If it had not done so, Japanese consumers would have bought the imported goods which were more attractive than home-produced goods.

Slow liberalisation of trade and under-estimation of competitiveness

That liberalisation of trade had not been accompanied by any perceptible increase in the sales of foreign manufactures could be attributed to the impressive improvement in quality of home-produced goods and reductions in their costs of production. The liberalisation was, however, postponed so that

[61]

Japanese manufacturers could become fully competitive with those of Western countries. To put it in another way, the government took liberalisation stage by stage so that Japanese manufacturers would not lose domestic markets in competition with imports.

Nevertheless, neither the government nor manufacturers were confident that domestic goods would be competitive enough with imports after liberalisation. In this sense both the government and manufacturers under-estimated their competitiveness. (I do not know whether their under-estimating of competitiveness was a kind of strategy in order to delay liberalisation or not. But it seems to have been real. When the Bank of Japan was keeping the yen from rising against the dollar immediately after the 'Nixon shock' of 1971, even a leading steel company seriously worried that the export of steel to the US would be impossible if the yen were allowed to appreciate in terms of the dollar.) It seems to me that this attitude forced Japanese manufacturers to make more efforts to improve their productive efficiency and the quality of their goods. I myself always felt that the government was too slow in liberalising imports.

As home-produced goods became competitive with imports, the market for imports tended to become limited to high-quality goods or specialities, the demand for which is inelastic in response to changes in price. Naturally importers did not reduce their prices in yen when the yen appreciated against dollars or pounds. But the demand for these goods might be price-elastic at prices slightly higher than those of home-produced goods.[1]

6. *Is distribution inefficient?*

Some part, at least, of the difference between the f.o.b. and the retail prices of imported manufactures can be attributed to their low price-elasticity; how much 'inefficiency' of distribution contributes to the difference between f.o.b. and retail prices is uncertain. And it is not always clear in what sense

[1] The department stores in Tokyo sell Burberry's all-cotton trench coats for twice as much as in London in terms of the current exchange rate. Quite a few Japanese tourists buy 'Burberry' or 'Aquascutum' coats in London. Their retail prices in London are higher than those of Japanese high-quality coats by probably 20 to 30 per cent. If they were sold at prices which moderately exceeded those of home-produced goods, the quantity sold would be much larger than at present, though gross sales revenue might not necessarily be larger.

distribution is inefficient. There is no reason why distribution systems should not differ from one manufacturer to another. Even the British practice of relying on sole agents might not necessarily be unsatisfactory.

From my personal experience, marketing and information factors are more important than an ambiguous notion of 'inefficiency'. It seems to me that Japanese consumers do not get enough information about imported manufactures except those of world-famous brands or those sold by aggressive sales campaigns. If it is profitable to sell imported manufactures, why do not the agents make more efforts to sell them?

I used the 'Garrard' record-player turntable which I bought in the US in 1962 for 13 years. The agent in Tokyo kept replacement parts in stock. In 1975 I bought the 'BSR' turntable with autochanger; I have been satisfied with it. But very few Japanese know of 'BSR' products.[1] A notable case of aggressive selling campaigns is that of Procter & Gamble, the American detergent manufacturer, which has successfully invaded the Japanese market through aggressive sales techniques such as advertising and undercutting retail prices. Some Japanese manufacturers have complained of P & G's price undercutting as 'predatory dumping'. Whether or not this is so is debatable. The leading Japanese manufacturer has been able to compete with P & G. Naturally enough, the competition has been welcomed by Japanese consumers.

7. Are imports impeded by conglomerates?

It is very hard to say whether or not the kind of 'discrimination' referred to by Professor Allen on pages 38-39 is 'unfair'. In addition to Professor Allen's explanations of 'unfair discrimination', two more observations may be made.

The first concerns the risk of depending upon overseas suppliers (particularly of engineering components). Japanese manufacturers, notably of motor cars, have tried to reduce the costs of their inventories (stocks) of components, particularly where their assembly plants are located near large concentrations of consumers such as Tokyo and other big cities. Since the price of land is extremely high, they have tended to economise on warehouse space for components. Most components are brought into the assembly plants from their suppliers in

[1] [Some Japanese equipment is fitted with 'BSR' turntables for sale in Britain. —ED.]

appropriate-sized lots for assembly lines to minimise costs of production. If the prices of components supplied by overseas manufacturers are low enough to compensate for the additional costs incurred in holding an inventory, Japanese manufacturers might shift from domestic to overseas suppliers.

Emphasis on flexibility of supply

In addition, Japanese manufacturers place a high value upon the flexibility of domestic suppliers in adjusting themselves to the requirements of their customers. The extent of flexibility probably depends upon the terms of the contract between purchasers and suppliers. The longer the term of contract and the more favourable the bargain, the more flexible is the adjustment of suppliers. This kind of flexibility or adaptability may, of course, be peculiar to Japanese business.[1]

Nevertheless, if Japanese manufacturers found that purchasing imported components was more advantageous than depending upon domestic products, taking costs in the broad sense to include not only apparent prices of components but also non-pecuniary or uncompensated services rendered by suppliers, they would switch the purchase of components from domestic to overseas suppliers.

Life-time employment and labour management efficiency

The second explanation might be more difficult for overseas manufacturers to understand. Conglomerates have many subsidiary companies which engage in supplying components or in distributing the parent company's manufactures. The parent transfers its employees who reach or are reaching retiring age to subsidiary companies in order to maintain a supply of senior staff positions to which younger employees can be promoted. Usually those who are transferred are paid as much as or perhaps less than they were before retiring from the parent company.[2] By this practice conglomerates are able

[1] When purchasers of components want the suppliers to increase supplies in accordance with an increase in production of finished goods, the component suppliers will adapt themselves to increase their production almost instantly, if possible, even if it entails over-time or holiday work. Whenever the relationship between a purchaser and a supplier is good in this sense, this kind of co-operation between them is possible.

[2] This is true only for employees whose labour productivity is unsatisfactory in comparison with wages and salaries paid before they retired from the parent company.

to maintain efficiency of labour management as a whole. Consequently it would be worthwhile for conglomerates to place their orders with subsidiary companies if the purchase prices of components were not considerably higher than those of overseas suppliers. Probably it would be profitable even for conglomerates to make cross-subsidies in the short term, though these cross-subsidies would be very limited. If their subsidiary companies became loss-making because of inefficiency or changes of market structure, conglomerates would close them down.

Conglomerates are private undertakings which are always seeking profits, and they will never permanently protect chronically loss-making companies. Even if conglomerates are monopolistic they would not sustain chronically loss-making subsidiaries in the long run, because if their monopolistic power is strong enough, subsidiaries can be kept from loss-making and no cross-subsidisation is then required.

8. On 'A VERDICT'[1]

(i) 'Complex distributive system'

Even among the Japanese there are some who say that the Japanese distributive system is complex. I do not see in what sense this is so. Certainly there still are traditional commission merchants (*tonya* in Japanese) which often play a two-fold role, that of wholesaler and of financier. Western critics probably pay more attention to other specific characteristics of the Japanese distributive system. But every country has its own social customs and history of business. Indeed, the Japanese themselves found difficulties in selling their manufactures when they tried to go into the US market because of the difference in trading practices between Japan and the US.[2] An executive of one of the leading trading companies told me that Japanese traders had studied the trading practices of the US and other Western countries in order to be successful in their exports.[3]

[1] Above, pp. 43-53.

[2] For some time after the war some Japanese manufacturers were exploited by American traders simply because they were ignorant of American trading practices. They were obliged to suffer considerable losses to improve their situation.

[3] In 1962 the executive of New York Nissan Motors Co., the agency responsible for importing Datsun cars into the US, explained their difficulties in selling Japanese cars there. I myself never anticipated, when I talked to him, that Japanese cars would ever sell so well.

[65]

In addition, he wondered why Western traders would not make the same kind of effort as the Japanese had done abroad in order to understand Japanese trading practices, if they wanted to sell their goods in Japan. Except for a few cases, such as those of beef and corn, import and distributive systems are not controlled and have recently been changing. The newly founded super chain stores have been growing rapidly by introducing trading and distributive systems different from traditional ones. Hence Japanese trading practices and distributive systems are not entirely rigid but capable of flexibility and change. Competition works even in the distribution industry.

(ii) *Economic growth and export strength*

The relationship between economic growth and export strength in Japan is very accurately analysed by Professor Allen. Two more observations might be made.

First, because of the complete destruction of plants by air raids, Japan could adopt the newest technology and also choose the best location for some industries, notably steel, when plants were reconstructed. In contrast with the American steel industry, 'new' construction rather than mere reconstruction enabled Japanese industries to be very efficient.

Secondly, the agrarian reform (which could only be done under the occupation) and post-war industrialisation not only raised the incomes of the Japanese people but also reduced income differentials. Consequently the purchasing power of the Japanese as a whole rose and this, in turn, expanded the domestic market, enabling industries such as the electrical appliance, electronics and automobile industries to adopt mass production.[1] In addition these industries were very competitive and they had to pay attention not only to the efficiency of production but also to the improvement of quality of goods. These characteristics of the domestic market contributed to foster Japan's export strength. The tremendous improvement in the productive efficiency of the motor industry is shown by Tables 2 and 3 (p. 71).

(iii) *Under-valuation of the yen*

The unexpected appreciation of the yen against the dollar

---

[1] During 1960-63 I was a graduate student in the US and owned a used car. I never expected to be able to own a car when I returned to Japan. But I was able to buy a new car in a few years because my income increased while cars became cheaper.

since the Autumn of 1977 has continued and, at the time of writing (March 1978), the yen is at its highest-ever value.

The Japanese Government has tried several times in the course of the appreciation of the yen to keep it from rising but has not succeeded. Generally speaking, the Japanese regard speculation as an undesirable practice which can and should be regulated by government. Sometimes government intervention aggravates the situation because it is the act of intervention itself which is the object of speculation. The government should take account of this point. According to Japanese newspapers, the Ministry of Finance has been considering restrictions on exports by law in order to stop the rise in the trade surplus. The government believes that this measure will reduce the trade surplus; the appreciation of the yen would therefore be avoided.[1] This sort of regulatory policy may be neither effective in avoiding speculation nor helpful in solving the problem in the long run.[2] The yen should be allowed to rise, since speculation continues only as long as the official rate does not reflect its market value.

(iv) *Are any other measures available?*

The expansion of expenditure on the infrastructure by the Japanese Government might be effective in increasing the rate of growth of the economy. But it will probably be less effective than in the 1950s and 1960s in increasing her imports, because the government expenditure multiplier has fallen. Most industries have surplus capacity, so no appreciable investment in manufacturing industries would be stimulated. An appreciable increase in consumption cannot be expected because, since the 'oil crisis', consumers' behaviour has changed: marginal propensity to consume has fallen from the high level of the years of rapid economic growth. The experience of depression after the 'oil crisis' has changed Japanese consumers' long persisting optimism about future incomes into pessimism.[3]

---

[1] *Nihon Keizai Shinbun*, 18 March, 1978. The Ministry of Finance is thinking of restricting exports by the government ordinance on control of export trade which was enforced in 1949 to stabilise the yen against the dollar.

[2] As long as Japan's competitive superiority in international markets is retained, successive enforcement and relaxation of government trade policy through these ordinances will simply stimulate speculation.

[3] This reversal of attitudes and behaviour was not recognised by the government. In 1976 it decreased personal income tax and paid back tax. But consumption did *not* increase. Also, contrary to the expectations of the government, the

[Continued on page 68]

Expansion of government provision of social welfare?

Another measure suggested by Professor Allen is the expansion of provisions for welfare (p. 50). Many people, including both foreign and Japanese scholars, attribute the high propensity to save of the Japanese to Japan's relatively sketchy social security services. However, the costs of the government social security services required to produce a given amount of welfare may differ from one country to another. For example, where families accept responsibility for the care of their elderly, governments are saved much of the high costs associated with old age. And the more welfare services are taken over by government, the more they cost. Higher *government* expenditure on social services does not therefore imply a higher level of welfare. Very often an increase in government expenditure on social welfare services is cancelled out by a decrease in personal (or household) expenditure. Certainly, for this reason, if the government takes over the responsibility for social welfare, households will expand their consumption and this *may* lead to an increase in imports.[1]

It is doubtful, however, if the Japanese people would be satisfied were the government to take over the responsibility for social welfare from the individual family. Young people, for instance, might then leave the responsibility for the welfare of the aged to the government. Under the traditional family system of the Japanese, the most desirable policy (from their viewpoint) would not be the mere expansion of provisions for welfare by the government. What should be sought is an

[*Continued from page 67*]

increase in government expenditure did not lead to an increase in consumption. The explanation may be that the downward adjustment of expected permanent income after the 'oil crisis' influenced the level of Japanese consumption expenditure. The Prime Minister, Mr Fukuda, expected the increase in consumption and investment expenditure brought about by the expansion of government expenditure to curtail the surplus in the balance of trade. But the economic structure after the oil crisis was no longer the same as before it. In addition, Mr Fukuda was very reluctant to adopt an inflationary economic policy since it was unpopular with the Japanese people. Consequently, the expansion of government expenditure was modest. The huge balance-of-trade surpluses in 1976 and 1977 were probably contrary to Mr Fukuda's wish. The expansion of public expenditure in late 1977 was undertaken by Mr Fukuda under diplomatic pressure abroad to which Mr Fukuda could assign responsibility for inflation should it occur.

[1] The government's taking of more responsibility for social welfare does not, of course, necessarily bring about an increase in consumption expenditure, because it requires increases in personal taxes which reduce disposable incomes.

optimal social welfare policy tailored to the requirements of the Japanese social system.

What the Japanese Government should do now

What should the Japanese Government do now? It should remove restrictions on imports as long as no significant involuntary unemployment is entailed, whether or not other countries adopt higher tariffs than Japan. To do so would benefit Japanese consumers.

Finally, I want to examine the reasons why the Japanese Government has been so reluctant to liberalise imports. The Japanese Government and people are not so different from others. Like the governments of other countries, the Japanese Government has to pay attention to the interests of industries which might suffer from liberalisation of imports. But it tends to over-estimate the losses they might suffer. It is natural for the government of a country to be reluctant to adopt measures which might damage the interests of its industries. The Japanese Government is no exception. It tends to take action when diplomatic pressure becomes strong, not because it tries to protect domestic industries as much as possible but because it can pass responsibility for the damage to the countries which put diplomatic pressure on Japan. Otherwise the government or the parties in power would lose popularity with voters. Japanese consumers certainly welcome liberalisation of imports, but they hesitate to demand that the government promote import liberalisation when they are told, whether rightly or not, that liberalisation would adversely affect small enterprises and their employees. This kind of tendency seems to me to be common to every country.

I am very much afraid that Japan may adopt the same attitude towards developing countries which are catching up with her as that now being adopted by Western countries towards Japan.

APPENDIX

TABLE I

STRUCTURE OF WAGES & SALARIES, WAGES & SALARIES IN REAL TERMS, AND PRODUCTIVITY OF LABOUR: JAPAN, 1973 TO 1976

(Rate of change (%) compared with previous year)

	1973 FY	1974 FY	1975 FY	1976 FY	1975 FY				1976 FY			
					Apr. June	July Sept.	Oct. Dec.	Jan. Mar.	Apr. June	July Sept.	Oct. Dec.	Jan. Mar.
Wages and Salaries in												
Cash (*Total*)	23·5	27·4	9·8	12·1	5·7	12·6	7·8	13·7	13·8	10·7	12·9	11·1
Regular W. & S.	19·6	25·9	13·0	12·5	12·8	11·5	12·7	15·1	14·0	12·6	12·4	11·2
Scheduled	19·3	30·5	13·7	10·3	16·4	13·0	12·6	13·4	11·2	10·3	10·2	9·6
Overtime Payments etc.	22·0	−11·2	4·1	41·8	−23·0	−4·4	14·2	40·4	55·5	42·9	39·0	29·6
Bonuses	36·1	31·4	1·1	11·0	−20·5	15·0	1·1	−13·8	12·9	6·3	13·6	8·1
Real Wages & Salaries	6·5	4·5	−0·5	2·6	−6·8	2·0	−0·3	4·4	4·0	0·8	2·8	1·7
Productivity of Labour	17·9	−5·2	0·8	13·3	−6·2	−2·5	2·0	10·9	13·8	14·4	15·0	10·4
Costs of Wages	4·8	34·3	8·9	−1·0	12·7	15·5	5·7	2·5	0·0	−3·2	−1·8	0·6

FY = Fiscal year (1 April to 31 March).

Notes (1) Source: The Ministry of Labour and Japan Productivity Centre.
(2) Total Wages & Salaries in Cash = Regular Wages & Salaries + Bonuses.
(3) Real Wages & Salaries (Index) = Total Wages & Salaries in Cash (Index)/CPI.
(4) Costs of Wages (Index) = Total Wages & Salaries in Cash (Index)/Labour Productivity (Index).

TABLE 2

INTERNATIONAL AUTOMOBILE INDUSTRY: PRODUCTIVITY OF LABOUR, 1955 TO 1973

(No. of vehicles produced per employee per year)

	1955	1965	1973
Japan	1·2	7·4	12·2
USA	11·1	13·9	14·9
W. Germany	3·9	7·1	7·3
France	3·6	6·1	6·8
UK	4·2	5·8	5·1
Italy	3·0	7·4	6·8

Notes (1) Source: Central Policy Review Staff, *The Future of the British Car Industry,* HMSO, 1975.

(2) Employees include those of industries of components and parts; clerical employees also included.

(3) Number of automobiles produced adjusted according to size of cars and kinds of vehicles.

TABLE 3

LABOUR PRODUCTIVITY INDEX OF THE JAPANESE AUTOMOBILE INDUSTRY, 1965 TO 1975

	Sales per Employee ('000 yen)	Tangible fixed assets per employee ('000 yen)	Gross value added per employee ('000 yen)	Index of Labour Productivity (1970=100)
1965	8,698	2,302	2,055	—
1970	15,783	3,424	3,085	100
1971	17,708	3,955	3,452	109
1972	19,716	3,884	3,915	126
1973	22,205	4,122	4,196	145
1974	24,588	4,755	4,071	136
1975	28,677	5,042	5,059	150

Source: Japan Productivity Centre & MITI.

QUESTIONS FOR DISCUSSION

1. Describe Japan's international trade in the 1950s.

2. What are the differences between the pattern of Japan's exports before the war and today?

3. Distinguish between the three different kinds of dumping.

4. How accurate are the accusations that Japan has been engaged in wholesale dumping? Do you think that dumping can be justified?

5. What is meant by the phrase 'administrative guidance'?

6. Why do you think Britain has not benefited by 'administrative guidance'?

7. What was the Sumikin case and what does it tell us about the structure of the Japanese economy?

8. Why do you think Japan's export performance has outstripped that of other countries in the Western world?

9. Do you think the accusations of trade discrimination by Japan against foreign importers are 'fair'? What is meant by 'fair'?

10. Why did Japan liberalise her trade policy in the 1960s and 1970s and what restrictions remain?

FURTHER READING

British Overseas Trade Board, *British Successes in Japan,* London, 1976.

Corbet, Hugh, *Trade Strategy in the Asia-Pacific Area,* Allen & Unwin, London, 1970.

Corbett, Jenny, *The European Community's Trade with Japan— Issues and Implications,* Australia-Japan Economic Relations Research Project, Australian National University, Canberra, 1978.

Henderson, D. F., *Foreign Enterprise in Japan,* University of North Carolina Press, 1977.

Hunsberger, W. S., *Japan and the United States in World Trade,* Harper and Row, New York, 1964.

Japan Economic Research Centre, *Pacific Trade and Development,* Tokyo, 2 vols., 1968 and 1969.

Japan Information Centre, *British Trade with Japan,* London, 1977.

Kitamura, Hiroshi, *Choices for the Japanese Economy,* Royal Institute of International Affairs: Chatham House, 1976.

Kojima, Kiyoshi, *Japan and a Pacific Free Trade Area,* Macmillan, London, 1971.

——, *Japan and a New World Order,* Croom Helm, London, 1977.

Lockwood, W. W., (ed.), *The State and Economic Enterprise in Japan,* Princeton University Press, Princeton, N.J., 1965.

Ohkawa, K., and Rosovsky, H., *Japanese Economic Growth,* Stanford University Press, Stanford, California, 1973.

Nishiyama, Chiaki, and Allen, G. C., *The Price of Prosperity: Lessons from Japan,* Hobart Paper 58, Institute of Economic Affairs, London, 1974.